"Michael Wright makes a compelling case that most companies and senior managers will have to significantly up their game to compete in the coming years. This book provides keen insight for strategic planners, but will probably have the greatest value for operating managers who need to lead large organizations in new directions. His prescription to build critical mass by mobilizing intangible assets and recognizing that innovation has become the "ante" in many industries, reinforced by sharp knowledge management, is both deeply practical and convincingly argued."
—*Nathaniel J. Mass, former Professor of Management at the M.I.T. Sloan School; Managing Director, N.J. Mass Associates, Inc. NYC*

"Speed. Agility. Foresight. If you think your business has enough of these traits, you may want to think again after reading *The New Business Normal*. In his book, Mr. Wright reminds us that we are entering a hyper-competitive business era where fast, flexible, forward-thinking organizations are the only ones that stand a chance."
—*Jeff Loomis, President/CEO, The Loomis Group*

THE NEW BUSINESS NORMAL

THE PERIL AND PROMISE OF NEW GLOBAL REALITIES

MICHAEL W. WRIGHT

WITH WALTER J. FERGUSON

KNOWLEDGE MANAGEMENT PRESS
CHASKA, MN

Published by Knowledge Management Press
3500 Lyman Blvd.
Chaska, MN 55318

Publisher's Cataloging-in-Publication Data
Wright, Michael W.
The new business normal : [the peril and promise of new global realities]. — [Chaska, MN : Knowledge Management Press, 2005]
p. ; cm.
ISBN: 0-9766254-0-7
Includes bibliographical references.
1. Success in business. 2. Industrial management. 3. Organizational behavior. I. Title. II. Ferguson, Walter J.
HF5386 .W75 2005
650.1—dc22   2005-921711

Book production and coordination by Jenkins Group, Inc. www.bookpublishing.com
Interior design by Debbie Sidman
Cover design by Chris Rhoads

Printed in the United States of America
09 08 07 06 05 • 5 4 3 2 1

Dedicated to Miller Bonner
The Best Friend a Man or a Golf Cart Ever Had
To: Maurine, Matthew, Anne, & Isabella Wright
and
The Ferguson Grandchildren
Tyler, Lotus, Blade, Jasmine, & Ryann

CONTENTS

ACKNOWLEDGMENTS

Without the support and many contributions of Walter Ferguson, this book would not have happened. For his contributions to the content, verbal sparring, and countless hours of dialogue, I cannot thank him enough. To Jerry Kurz for having the foresight and trust to let me stretch my skills early on. To Pete Simone for having the guts to throw me into the business survival fight of a lifetime and stay at my back to the end. To Wayne Bongard and Dan Quernemoen for their examples of character and courage. To Vince Huntoon, Art Smith, Jim Moore, Randy Willig, Dick Dryden, Bob Yarborough, Rob Williamson, and Dan Rose, who all taught me how to be a marketer, businessman, and friend. To Matthew Miau for his unparalleled demonstration of hospitality, generous gift of time and a tour of his Chinese operations, and friendship. To Team Entegris, led by CEO Jim Dauwalter and its gifted Chairman Stan Geyer, for tolerating my attempt to create a corporate society and business frameworks capable of dealing with the new business normal. I'd specifically like to note my appreciation for the support of Alden Sutherland, Anna Anderson, and Cindy Schmieg of Entegris, Inc. along with Matt Kucharski of Padilla, Speer, Beardsley Public Relations.

And to my children who have inspired me to write this book. Hopefully, this book will provide some insights about a world you will inherit.

May it add light to your way.

Michael W. Wright

PREFACE

By Michael W. Wright with Walter J. Ferguson

"The New Normal isn't where you wait for the next boom. It's about the rest of your life."
—Roger McNamee (*Fast Company* magazine, Welcome to the First year of the Rest of our Lives, May 2003)

This book is ***not*** the typical business book genre of "twelve steps to survive and thrive" but instead is a point of view regarding the business landscape where the world can quickly make companies, their products and people much less valuable. Nor is this book about functional excellence like "winning product management strategy." Instead, it is a clarion call to managements and boards of directors who need conviction to renew and rethink. It is addressed to all in business and government who mistakenly see economic life as a location, a position, or a perpetuation of the past rather than as a journey. We are not attempting to win a Nobel Prize in economics for original thought. Rather, we have combined our executive experiences in global high-technology businesses to characterize the most important challenges and issues affecting corporate survival and prosperity in the ensuing years. In this endeavor, we have drawn on many informed sources for content and corroboration.

The global landscape we have painted seems intractable; we have embraced the term first introduced into common business use by Roger McNamee, the "New Normal." This landscape is harsh and forbidding, one that will render useless any attempt to palliate through cliché or dumbing down through generic format. We offer much content along a "how-to" path and cite many examples of successful navigation. But the main mission of the book is to map the scale (size) and scope (diversity) of the landscape. Any organization has to have a clear understanding of its present to divine its future. What we have done is illuminate the time and terrain between today and tomorrow.

This book was written because we, including you, are living in a permanently changed world. This fact does not escape most readers. But we feel we have put together in one volume a comprehensive and readable view of the most significant components of global change and leverage affecting corporate management. Our purview is perhaps the **first** of its kind. Our career backgrounds of being at the leading and sometimes bleeding edge of technology have given us the perspective to view our subject from the greatest enabler of all change, high technology. High technology is both the nucleus and ripple of change on a global scale that calls for new acceptance, new organization models, new priorities, and new preparation.

The changes we are seeing represent a combination of elements that have put in place a new set of realities that has forever changed how business is created, conceived, and conducted. The pace is faster, the challenges are bigger, and the opportunities are almost unimaginably greater than ever before. There is a disconcerting side to these changes that is inescapable. Regardless of the number of excellent business books that have touched on possible solutions to individual components of the new business normal, there is no easy answer, no magic bullet, no self-help book that will define your individual path through the landscape the new business normal realities have created. In our opinion, to most companies, the totality of the landscape is unexplored.

The structure of the book is a sense of gestalt, an integral system and pattern of thoughts that create a functional unit. Chapters are comprehensible in and of themselves and can be read in order of their topicality and interest. We recommend that the Introduction and Chapter One be read first. The writing is often declarative, and we expect that critical thinkers will sometimes find exceptions from their own experience in the vast expanse of the new business normal. True to our executive heritage, we have opted for summary discussion rather than scholarly examination. Walt, as contributing author, and I have combined our senior management experience of more than 60 years to provide insights, suggestions, and successes that we hope will become golden placers that you can use as you navigate in the months and years ahead.

INTRODUCTION

The New Business Normal Realities

"The growing complexity of our times makes certainty about any move or any position much more precarious. And in this networked world where information moves at the speed of light and 'truth' mutates before our eyes, certainty changes and speeds off at equivalent velocity."
—Margaret Wheatley, in essay "Willing to be Disturbed," from *Kaos Pilot A-Z* by Uffe Ubæk (Aarhus, Denmark: KaosCommunication, 2003)

"We are in one of those great historical periods that occur every 200 to 300 years when people don't understand the world anymore, when the past is not sufficient to explain the future."
—Peter Drucker

The new business normal is made up of sea changes in the business world around us. Success has become temporary for the many and a test of those who have enjoyed it in the past (e.g., dot-coms). In the transition from the old normal to the new, a stream of dynamics has redefined the business environment we have known all our lives.

Fasten your seat belt!

- Knowledge workers in a corporation may outlive the corporation itself.
- Change is accelerating beyond the fundamental ability of organizations to anticipate it.
- The time to act is when the need and opportunity first become apparent.
- Acting on inklings will become a key to surviving the speed of change.
- Waiting for management "handles" like budgets, formal development teams, or the arrival of a competitor's new product will limit market participation.
- The rule of three prevails.
- The percentage of business available in pure competition is shrinking in many industries.
- The overcapacity of goods and services in most markets in the developed world has made any more than three offerings meaningless to the consumer.
- *Value has migrated to the experience and away from the product enabling the experience.* For example, a cell phone without a subscription is a paperweight. Consumers want the value of the experience and not the responsibility or burden of product ownership. Witness the growth of car leasing.
- *Customers don't like clutter or visible complexity.* They have little time or interest in constant experimentation once their needs are met. Instruction manuals, assembly instructions, and maintenance guidelines have become burdens and are primarily legal posturing.
- The new business normal has seen a major change in margin structure.
  - There are countless global, cost-denominated competitors accessible through a click.
  - Overcapacity, too much competition, and no pricing power describe most industries.
  - Users and customers are more knowledgeable than ever about their needs and the value proposition of what they are buying.
  - Margin restructuring has become obligatory as corporate partnerships and joint ventures gain traction as a way to improve return on assets and broaden economic risk taking.
- *Product differentiation has powered brand dominance, yet it will not be enough left unattended or unexpanded.* Product differentiation was so strong for the Xerox brand that it became a verb, yet the success of Xerox has proved temporary. Starbucks defined what being in the coffee business really means. They broke most of the myths of what constituted "good" coffee perpetuated by the vested interests of major food companies. Today, Starbucks is virtually

a seal of approval for the hip and trendy. The new Blackberry describes an entire functionality and has trumped a very crowded field of players and product options. Expect much more differentiation as global brands emerge from China and as the Koreans, Taiwanese, Russians, Indians, Malaysians, and others all gain economic footing.

- *A broadscale phenomenon of the new business normal is that organizational economic security is gone for individuals, corporations, and governments.* For example, how many companies have underfunded pension programs? Ford, UAL, and Delta quickly come to mind. How many retirees are making daily choices between nourishing meals or the medicines they need? How many states are finally organizing to create high-paying jobs, some 60 years after the semiconductor was invented, just to bolster their tax base?

- *People differences in the new business normal are between those who know and those who don't know rather than between the haves and the have-nots of yesterday.* Individuals need to invest in themselves. Education is expensive, but ignorance is more expensive. The offset to insecurity is knowledge. The knowledge worker's competence will provide a transferable safety net as companies and governments rise and fall.

- *Personal time is gone.* It takes more time to maintain your knowledge, your skills, your networks, and your awareness of global conditions. Time loss comes with empowered and leaner organizations. In a 24/7/365 economy, time can no longer be parceled into convenient periods between personal and business. The new business normal is disruptive to the social fabric of the past and is characterized by families having fewer children and mixed gender roles.

- *Dual-income households are an economic necessity.* This is driving a greater wedge between those who know and those who don't. Half in jest, I offer that economic pressures are so relentless that society's new "trophy wife" is a Ph.D. from China with her own business.

- *Economically, we are a long way from the day when people are measured and rewarded on the value their thoughts bring to humanity.* And that means a shift is developing in how individual contributions to the corporation are treated. Reward and recognition are taking new forms: quality of life, flex hours, remote work locations, upgraded hardware, database access, flatter organizational models, etc.

- *Low-stress family life is nonexistent.* The average work week has increased, competition for access to higher education keeps nonworking hours fully occupied, and the plethora of fast food, fast service, and fast diagnosis businesses merely reflect a response to stresses families face in the new business normal. Children, by default, are in danger of becoming second-class citizens, being shuffled from activity to activity and caregiver to caregiver as parents seek economic security and quiet space.

- *Amoral behavior is on the rise.* A sense of irresponsibility and a general lack of conscience pervade many communities. Gangs, latch-key kids, Internet cheating, and tuning in to tune out are popular methods of coping. The computer game—the be-all and end-all baby-sitter, mind sitter, thought filler, and fat builder—has replaced the community and direct human interaction. More people think it's okay to cheat on their taxes. The underground economy now exceeds $1 trillion.

- *The base level of human existence is at a higher level of anxiety for all.* In addition, there are natural laws and body rhythms that are not in sync with some of what technology offers. Planes take us to every corner of the planet. Unfortunately, only adrenalin keeps pace with the assault on our circadian rhythms. The result is anxiety.

- *Individuals are exclusive and are becoming less inclusive.* In public and private places, the individual is an island and can stay that way: iPod, Bose headsets, computer-based conversations, and home alone (the fastest growing segment of the population is single-person households). Cell phones connect but do not engage all the senses. The Internet connects to everyone but especially to those who hold similar tribal norms and seek anonymous relationships whether in the local neighborhood or across the globe. But businesses in the new business normal are just the opposite. Connectivity among the human family is becoming more and more through one's business life and through pop culture.

- *The arrogance of ego is not a proxy for entitlement.* Arrogance will be poisonous to leaders, organizations, colleagues, and subordinates. Achievement outside of individual sports will depend on the successful integration and marshalling of groups of varied interests. Corporations that act as though they are above the law wreak havoc on their constituents. Good corporate citizenship is good policy.

- *Great companies will learn to continuously morph (change to fit the environment) as dynamic organisms or perish.* Each and every person in the organization will need to develop additional skills and keep a very open view to the world as it changes around them. And that rate of change is accelerating.

- *Innovation is becoming the new business model as differentiation through manufacturing wanes.* Companies must learn morphing as a rigor versus a theory. Morphing will come through the use of more outside people, temporaries, consultants, executive committees, and boards with more international diversity.

- *The old reflex actions at crunch time to cut head count, cut advertising, and beat up on the suppliers are 180 degrees from the new business normal.* These old knee-jerk reactions to adverse changes in market direction will do nothing more than put the company at even greater risk by removing the assets that could be used to build its future through branding, new products, and new skill set development. The rearview mirror drivers will crash early and often—the past is no longer the beginning of the future.

- *Leadership in the new business normal will systematically deploy the right people, expand the brand, and seek a seamless integration of supply chains.*

- *Looking out the side window will not help with how to drive to the future either.* Companies and individuals must remain forward focused with more diligence than ever before. Mere scrutiny of events as they happen will not be sufficient. A receptivity to change predisposes the individual to anticipatory behaviors, a highly regarded attribute, as emphasis is placed on innovation and speed in the new business normal. As is true in most life-and-death stories, reaction time will be crucial if one is to survive and thrive.

- *Every business will be successful until it makes mistakes.* In the new business normal, mortal mistakes will be many, and the business models that break will be like Humpty Dumpty. As an example, students of the S Curve hold that at the point of discontinuity between technologies, product leadership changes 70 percent of the time, and survivability often goes with it. Diversification is a strategic defense, but it is increasingly difficult to execute because of barriers to entry in well-served markets.

- *Value will accrue to those organizations able to reward the whole person who comes to work and voluntarily gives over to the company his or her most precious assets: time and emotional commitment.* As humans spend

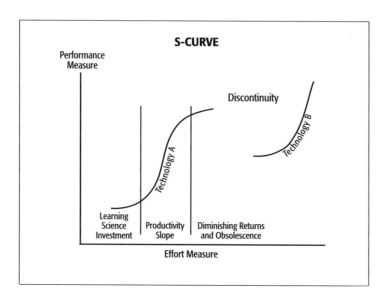

S-CURVE

Source: Preston G. Smith. *Developing Products in Half the Time: New Rules, New Tools* (New York: John Wiley & Sons, Inc. 1998)

more of their life engaged in the process of making a living, they will demand more satisfaction from their means of livelihood. Most experts agree that the new generations entering the workforce will be even more comfortable with the latest technology and will know how to use it in a culturally diverse workplace. The buzzword for this generation is "multitasking," with work and home life merging into one. Passion has to be inspired by management and has to burn brightly in each individual on the team. Apathy and indifference will kill engagement often and without mercy. The unsentimental judgment of the well-served marketplace will assure that only the swift and knowledgeable survive. An unengaged workforce is unable to learn and move quickly. Said another way, talent without discipline is waste.

- *Shareholder concerns will become a residual of values-driven management able to engage people across cultures and borders. The companies with the most engaged people will win.*

- *As more information is collated and codified in greater volumes and with greater speed, there is a risk to all employees of becoming ignorant at an accelerating pace.*

- *The growth of information is evidenced by the rapid growth of Web sites on the Internet.* Researchers at the Online Computer Library Center (OCLC) claim that the Web now contains some 8.4 million unique sites, compared to 7.1 million in 2000 and 4.6 million in 1999.

- *What you have created is not yours to keep.* There are countless well-trained brains graduating across the globe able to copy, surmise, and surprise. Reverse engineering is no longer a black art but a well-tuned and fully supported business discipline. Governments have complicity too! Until recently, all imports into China were regulated to go through indigenous trading companies that were known sources of pirating and cloning.

- *Target marketing is the most direct path to the customer in the new business normal.* What's changed is that social and economic profiling of the consumer is now the domain of the mass retailer. According to an article in the July 12, 2004, issue of *Business Week*, McDonald's now devotes less than a third of its U.S. marketing budget to television, compared with two-thirds five years ago. Money that used to go for network spots now pays for closed-circuit sports programming piped into ethnic bars and ads in custom-published magazines and in-store retail video networks. "We are a big marketer," says M. Lawrence Light, McDonald's chief marketing officer. "We are not a mass marketer."

- *Through bar coding, point-of-purchase data accumulation, and zip code census, retailers are amassing invaluable information regarding brand preference, price elasticity, turnover, and regionality.* And just wait until radio frequency identification (RFID) becomes mainstream. It'll be to bar code what the computer was to the typewriter. Manufacturers are more dependent on the retail sales channel and the data it produces, while the retailer and end user have become more reliant on the brand pull and innovativeness of the manufacturer's product. These chains are tightening and becoming more interdependent.

The new business normal is a complex world far, far from the Jeffersonian ideal of self-sufficient gentlemen farmers and artisans. The new business normal is disruptive and harsh. Like it or don't, technology seldom goes backward. It goes forward, becoming more ramified and more arcane.

This book is not designed to be a complete "how to" or a proclamation of preaching "thou shall" and "thou shall not" in the wake of these many changes. It is, at its core, both an empirical and a philosophical examination of the way business transacts in the new business normal. It endeavors to take stock of what it means to thrive today and tomorrow. It is a text of observations and possible strategies gathered directly, indirectly, through osmosis, and by the experience of being at the center of dynamic global organizations. It is my hope that it will encourage progressive and pragmatic corporate and career behaviors. The changes fostered in the new business normal continue to resonate with me, and I have been privileged to see pioneering business practices take shape and rapidly emerge.

A lifelong fascination of mine with business organizations has led to the writing of this book. The inner voice of my experiences tells me not only that the changes in the new business normal are here to stay but also that they are being swiftly adopted around the globe. They will continue to reach across industry lines on a global scale, more quickly than anyone can imagine. I hope you find the ensuing chapters as relevant and inspiring as I do; it is certainly my pleasure to share them with you. It's not your "father's Oldsmobile" anymore; it, like the old normal, is gone.

WARNING

Prepare to be uncomfortable. Be ready to discover and reaffirm tensions that are not yet resolved. Get excited about what you can do to meet the challenges of the new business normal and succeed.

ONE

Permanent Change

"The future is already here . . .
It's just unevenly distributed." —Anonymous

The new business normal realities have converged to hit us like water from a fire hose. The changes we are experiencing in our global and regional economies are equivalent to permanent sea-level changes on our economic shores.

Our economy today is more conceptual than physical. Virtual factories work. Seven-by-twenty-four global enterprises exist. Everyone is connected to everyone. The networked organization of "networked organizations" is making a profit. Information technology is now a competitive advantage. Manufacturing differentiation is nearly nonexistent. The presence, attitude, and role of China have irreversibly changed the global marketplace, potentially for centuries to come. Speed is the function of the reduction of transaction time and is no longer a debatable metric. When things happen is becoming more important than how they happen. Consumers want the experience of a product or service but not the ownership. A darkening environment of debt, both public and private, pervades markets. Proximity to customers and lower-cost manufacturing has created a politically unpopular need to globally reposition operations. Being close to the customer is more than a turn of a phrase. Populations in developed countries are not reproducing themselves, and workforces are aging and retiring. The noise level of data is deafening. The competitive bar has risen, powered by an unprecedented era of continuous improvement across all business activities that focused on the productivity of human resources. The business landscape is both confined and borderless. Change accelerates every minute of every day. A different kind of leadership is required because the past is no longer prologue and the future is not what we remember it to be. E-commerce, the vagabond knowledge worker, outsourcing, and temporary workforces raise the question of the very survival of the corporation. The synchronous agglomeration of these elements could constitute a "company." These elements, when combined, have created a paradigm shift of unprecedented significance, sufficient and extensive enough to call it THE NEW BUSINESS NORMAL.

Clearly, we have entered this "new normal"—and a new set of standard assumptions and practices has become essential to the way business is handled, planned, and managed. Without even realizing it, people have begun to talk about the changes in the way products are bought, sold, and even defined as products. The use of the phrase "the new normal" in the business vernacular is indicative of the heady pace that technology has provided. The very fact that phrases such as "the new normal" make their way into contemporary usage at all simply proves that the mindset and standards of business have changed.

Boardrooms are no longer rubber-stamping the past. Rather, in the reality of a global marketplace, they are relying on innovative and thoughtful management teams to differentiate and lead the enterprise forward. Companies have been forced to expand the space around their product and become demonstratively involved with the success of their customers. There has been a rebirth of focus on innovation as being critical to business growth, perhaps even its survival. Businesses are pondering how they can simultaneously reduce costs, increase competitiveness, hang on to customers, and foster innovation in a global marketplace that can, at any moment, undersell them based on price point alone.

The new business normal is both a practice and an idea. It captures the essence of a new way to look philosophically at business life as it undergoes the most rapid change in history. From reengineering to servant leadership, these practices and ideas are currently at work all around the globe, and they are affecting all businesses, regardless of size or geographic location. This new mode of business is at once fluid, global, electrifying, and deeply competitive. Organizations that survive in this new environment will adapt and reflect these qualities in their core missions and daily practices. Collectively, these streamlined and attentive organizations will push the limits of technology to what is possible, what is plausible, and what perseveres.

Resilience

"It usually takes a performance crisis to prompt the work of renewal. Rather than go from success to success, most companies go from success to failure and then, after a long, hard climb, back to success. Resilience refers to a capacity for continuous reconstruction. It requires innovation with respect to those organizational values, processes, and behaviors that systematically favor perpetuation over innovation."

—Gary Hamel (Harvard Business Review, "The Quest for Resilience," Sept. 2003)

While the new business normal resembles a frontier of sorts, there are few lone cowboys out on the range these days. Everything an enterprise does is part and parcel of what the world is doing at large. Interconnectivity is no longer a science fiction phrase or futuristic. Those poised for prosperity already know this, and as I write, they are growing and succeeding because they have learned how to make the new business normal work to their advantage. They are wise to regional specialties, economies of scale, IT core competence, and competitive measures such as asset redeployment and worker passion.

These alert corporations have come to recognize a set of fundamental changes in business. Customers aren't just looking for a product or a service anymore—they're looking for an experience. Consumer trend watchers such as Yankelovich and Partners and NOP Worldwide clearly document the trend. We don't have glasses anymore—we have eyewear. We don't have used cars—we have preowned vehicles. We don't have soap—we have facial cleansers. That sales guy? He's now a sales consultant. Need more evidence? Among the top business books over the past years are titles such as *The Experience Economy*, by Joseph Pine and James Gilmore; *The Substance of Style*, by Virginia Postrel; and *Trading Up, The New American Luxury*, by Michael Silverstein and Neal Fiske.

In the new business normal, customers have more choices than ever. They are willing to pay for what they need, but what they need is continuously changing as they adapt to the pace, pattern, and pressures of the new business normal. They want a product that will grow with them. They aren't just looking for a dynamic brand that makes them feel good but one that will cater to their needs and enable them to accomplish their own goals and meet their own challenges over time. In this new landscape, customers resemble more of a business partner than an occasional client, and leading corporations have invested in their customers' viewpoints to a level of codestiny that might very well have been unimaginable just 10 years ago.

While succeeding in the new business normal means uncovering the hidden terrain of profitability, it also means returning to some of the business know-how too quickly abandoned during the euphoria of the dot-com bubble. Management, celebrated in the popular press, became confused with performance. In the new business normal, management teams, who are able to achieve long-term and economically relevant goals, are values driven and legacy minded. They will regain boardroom favor over short-term, cost-focused marionettes of Wall Street. It is heartening to see these fundamentally important behaviors reestablish themselves as key frameworks in the new business normal.

In the new business normal, the greatest assets available to achieve and sustain longevity are human resources. The new business normal requires cultivating the full potential of people from every geographic region, at every age and skill level, and for every opportunity. It requires investing in people as much as in automation and R&D.

The new business normal is a game of continuous review of balance. It is about balancing values, ethics, and accountability with aggressive innovation and lean practices.

It is about reassessing your company's relationship with all of its constituencies: customers, suppliers, employees, directors, competitors, analysts, investment bankers, universities, and communities. The way we communicate and do business has transformed everyone on the planet.

This atmosphere requires strong, dependable leaders willing to do the hard work. Business today demands leaders focused on the horizon who stimulate and create change rather than simply respond to it. It requires servant leaders who work toward a greater purpose than momentary share price or an option expiration date. Leaders are needed who influence the behaviors of people in a positive way by inspiring hope in their future and by training them for motivated performance in the present. These rare individuals will be key to a company's ability to navigate in the new business normal. Simultaneously, new business normal companies must become ever leaner and always more agile, and they must find ways to get their products to market at an unprecedented pace.

A company destined to survive has a thorough understanding of the challenges and practices of doing business in this contemporary climate and has a strong strategic, as well as tactical, mindset. Scale and scope do not happen overnight. Sustainable advantages must be maintainable beyond the life of the intellectual property that engendered them and secure enough to allow survival during transitions. The core capabilities of companies will derive from the intentional development of empowered people with greater depth, skills, and flexibility.

The new business normal is not a trend but a fork in the road. It is about recognizing the choices surrounding the future that cannot be extrapolated from either the past or the present. It is making decisions in many cases about an unknowable unknown. I believe we must constantly pay attention to what we are learning and look diligently for the insight we are accruing in our collective knowledge base. We must clear the road ahead of overwhelming noise and the associated clutter it entails.

Welcome to the new business normal. Are we having fun yet?

TWO

Critical Mass

Not big, but big enough

Much has been written about critical mass but not about its relevance to the survival of a company in a finite market space. Scope and scale combine to form critical mass, and because of them, the new business normal dispels a common misconception that innovation stems from small companies. Scope is the breadth of a company's capabilities. Existing and desired capabilities form the basis for growth through scope. Scale is the volume or number of iterations of the capabilities within scope. Companies with critical mass are able to effectively divert resources to new or problem markets and manage the factors of risk and opportunity better than small companies. More important, they are able to accelerate global market penetration rates because of their infrastructure and greater access to capital markets. The beginning seeds may come from smaller enterprises, but the critical mass of large companies gives innovation a commercial life. Lifestyle companies such as violin repair, handmade greeting cards, or custom-made sand wedges may enjoy high gross margins, but their unsupported growth potential in the new business normal will likely be small.

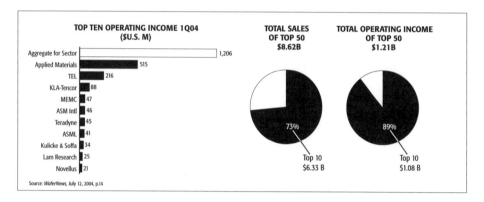

When you do the math in the above graphic describing the recent performance of the top 10 in the semiconductor equipment and materials market, you will find this leaves $130 million of operating income that can be invested in the future, and it

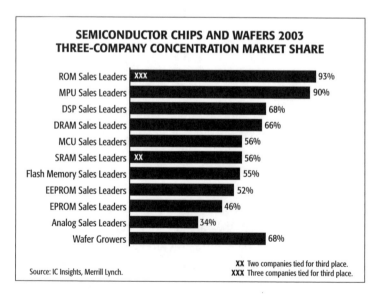

Oligopoly structure at work in the semiconductor and semiconductor equipment space.

must be divided among the remaining 40 players. In an industry that requires a 12 to 15 percent of sales annual investment in R&D, there is no way for these players to sustain a competitive position long term. This demonstrates clearly the value of critical mass. It is not size relative to all companies but size relative to the market space. Being a $1-billion company in a $50-billion market is not scale; being a $1-billion company in a $1.5-billion market is. Scale is also size relative to the next-larger company by market share in that space.

In a noninflationary global economy, most companies do not have pricing power. Low inflation should continue as emerging industrial countries, which represent nearly 70 percent of the world's population (Japan, Taiwan, Korea, China, India, Russia), continue to suppress pricing, focusing instead on market footing and keeping their vast populations employed. As can be seen from the following two illustrations, market leadership is rewarded disproportionately, a fact not lost on regional and national governments in the new business normal.

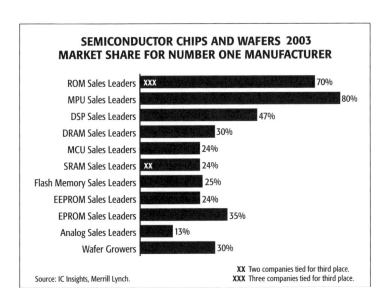

SEMICONDUCTOR CHIPS AND WAFERS 2003
MARKET SHARE FOR NUMBER ONE MANUFACTURER

ROM Sales Leaders — XXX — 70%
MPU Sales Leaders — 80%
DSP Sales Leaders — 47%
DRAM Sales Leaders — 30%
MCU Sales Leaders — 24%
SRAM Sales Leaders — XX — 24%
Flash Memory Sales Leaders — 25%
EEPROM Sales Leaders — 24%
EPROM Sales Leaders — 35%
Analog Sales Leaders — 13%
Wafer Growers — 30%

Source: IC Insights, Merrill Lynch.

XX Two companies tied for third place.
XXX Three companies tied for third place.

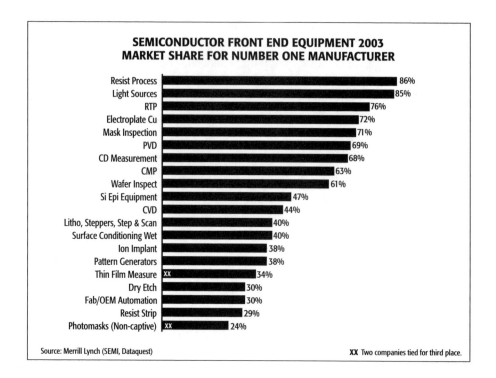

SEMICONDUCTOR FRONT END EQUIPMENT 2003 MARKET SHARE FOR NUMBER ONE MANUFACTURER

Resist Process	86%
Light Sources	85%
RTP	76%
Electroplate Cu	72%
Mask Inspection	71%
PVD	69%
CD Measurement	68%
CMP	63%
Wafer Inspect	61%
Si Epi Equipment	47%
CVD	44%
Litho, Steppers, Step & Scan	40%
Surface Conditioning Wet	40%
Ion Implant	38%
Pattern Generators	38%
Thin Film Measure	XX 34%
Dry Etch	30%
Fab/OEM Automation	30%
Resist Strip	29%
Photomasks (Non-captive)	XX 24%

Source: Merrill Lynch (SEMI, Dataquest)   **XX** Two companies tied for third place.

The ability to absorb ancillary costs in developed nations (e.g., health care, insurance, profit sharing, pension funding, and regulatory compliance) can be efficiently addressed only with size. Ford Motor Company, for example, is now paying more per vehicle for health care than for steel.

In the new business normal, scale matters. The ability to support continuous R&D separates the long-term players from those whose only horizon is the next technology node.

Small companies can show growth, but only large companies can create significant innovation. Looking at the capital structure, investor lists, and advisors of small companies who have reached commercial scale proves the point. Large company financial positions and executive participation are everywhere in evidence. If you can develop an idea and initialize the prototype as a small company, you will need additional capital to bring it to market, and that capital accrues to large companies that can commercialize ideas on a large scale.

In the new business normal, there are even fewer lone pioneers on the trail. New technical product generations today tend to come from large companies or coalitions of companies acting in partnership. It took DuPont to invent nylon. It took IBM to develop copper interconnect for semiconductors. Tomorrow it will take several consortia to commercialize nanotechnology. Partnerships in the new business normal also extend to government agencies, national laboratories, and university research efforts. Governments have recognized the need for critical mass. The interpretation and enforcement of antitrust statutes have been redefined and loosened. In the new business normal, "big business" is less the enemy in public policy. "Big" is not what it used to be.

DISTRIBUTED INNOVATION

Few companies can meet all their research goals alone. So the smart ones are adopting an "open" research model that allows them to pool some assets. Here's what that entails.

SCOURING THE GLOBE for useful innovations, rather than trying to invent everthing in-house

LICENSING INTELLECTUAL PROPERTY to other companies – in part to pay for outside research

FORGING TIES WITH UNIVERSITY LABS even if this means sharing prized intellectual-property rights

COURTING VENTURE-CAPITAL FUNDING and welcoming the discipline VCs impose

ENCOURAGING SPIN-OFFS that will pursue novel ideas and take risks

Source: Henry W. Chesbrough's Open Innovation, *BusinessWeek.*

Large companies will often underwrite the development of new technologies in smaller companies. Intel, for example, has invested billions in small company R&D projects that are in line with its strategic intent. Pharmaceutical companies have long followed a similar path.

In the new business normal, relative size, whether organic, networked, or virtual, becomes a necessary vehicle for sustainable economic value creation. But this advantage of scale is sustainable only if size is maintained by retaining company know-how over time. Management needs to be very flexible in balancing long-term

planning horizons with rapid scope adjustments. Today we ask, "Where is the margin going to come from?" In well-served markets, the answer seems to be "Not where it used to."

Critical mass enables the networking of multiple disciplines and supply chains to create significant economic advantages. I do not mean networking for the sake of attempting to be all things to all people, but rather having the ability to impact costs by virtue of scalability. Low cost is one of only two remaining ways to differentiate a company through manufacturing. The other is unique and extremely well-protected know-how. Unfortunately, whatever is newly developed in manufacturing processes seems to quickly diffuse to the competition through new technology, suppliers, or the high mobility of knowledge workers.

Critical mass is very much a necessity to be global. Most views of what "global" means come up short in the new business normal. Global does not mean exporting. To export means the company is involved with international trade. Nor does global mean having an overseas subsidiary in the model of a U.S. parent. This signifies the company has a foreign office. Global does mean having operations in locations that reflect the culture and customer needs of the host country and indigenous market. These operations have the look and feel of a native company in the host country but with a global brand promise. Global means that sales, service, operations management, community relations, and legal matters are all conducted locally.

The terms "foreign" and "domestic" lose their distinctions in the new business normal. The Chicago office is the same in stature, voice, and mind-set as the Bangkok office. The two just happen to be in different host countries. While each culture may have nuances that need to be appreciated, the overall mind-set of cooperation within the company tribe prevails. National thinking is replaced by transnational thinking as seamless flows of currencies around the globe have more impact than the political policies of any one government. Economic unions of countries with common cultural heritage allow less restricted economic activity among member nations, making moot points of their natural political borders. National currencies are giving way to new transnational currencies, such as the Euro, within world regions.

In the new business normal, mass and momentum remain related. If you're a Lilliputian, you might want to suck up to Gulliver.

THREE

Intangible Assets

The true competitive differentiators

In a nonaccounting sense, the defining assets of the new business normal include a skilled, knowledge-based workforce, corporate goodwill, brand recognition, customer relationships, intellectual property, and electronic data systems that can output business intelligence.

Add to these a first-rate process to design and introduce new products and a logistically efficient global supply chain. Together, these intangible assets have become the true competitive differentiators of the new business normal. The value of physical assets, from stately headquarters buildings to manufacturing facilities, which custom producers can equal or surpass, has diminished.

Corporate goodwill accrues over time. Therefore, being young and growing rapidly will not assure viability. In the new business normal, goodwill requires the demonstration of performance over time and implies positive customer behaviors exhibiting a preference for the company's brand.

This means corporate goodwill must be earned through a time warp of meaningful relationships with all of the company's constituents. It cannot be purchased. It implies trust and reliability, and once earned, goodwill becomes a force to sustain margins. Once lost, it is likely certain death.

Brand is probably the most important asset a company has. It is the company's currency to open, maintain, and control markets. It is the framework under which new products are contemplated, funded, developed, and introduced into the marketplace. Brand gives pricing power. Products sourced from certain regions of the world possess inherent brand promise (e.g., Swiss watches, English leather, Italian fabrics, and German cars). In the new business normal, regions must leverage the brand position given to them in the global marketplace. Going outside of the consumer mindset requires higher market development costs with commensurate risk—expect to spend some pioneering positioning money if you're going to market with English gourmet food, French automobiles, German lingerie, or Italian tower engineering.

THE WORLD'S 10 MOST VALUABLE BRANDS

RANK	BRAND	2002 BRAND VALUE ($ BILLIONS)
1	COCA-COLA	69.6
2	MICROSOFT	64.1
3	IBM	51.2
4	GE	41.3
5	INTEL	30.9
6	NOKIA	30.0
7	DISNEY	29.3
8	McDONALD'S	26.4
9	MARLBORO	24.2
10	MERCEDES	21.0

Source: Interbrand Corp., J.P. Morgan Chase & Co., as appeared in *BusinessWeek*, August 5, 2002.

Customer relationships are the ultimate marketing weapon. Mutuality with the customer is a profitability proposition over time. Past studies show that the longer a customer is retained, the more likely that the relationship is profitable. In the new business normal, a growing gross margin by customer is the most significant indicator of the health and duration of that relationship.

In the new business normal, a company will not let intermediaries such as distributors, brokers, or agents get between it and its customer. No doubt, these sales channels can be important conduits serving the small or upstart business, but they still have to offer value to exist. It is also true that companies producing commodities are often served well by intermediaries because local availability is central to marketing commodities. And xenophobia remains a fact of life in the global market where nationalistic customers will insist on indigenous contacts. However, because innovation rules in the new business normal, companies need a direct working relationship with their customers. This relationship will grow to where success is a mutual goal, and suppliers will likely share costs, facilities, and knowledge workers with their customers. Companies that come to mind exemplifying mutuality in their relationships with suppliers and customers are Dell and Saturn.

New organizational models for relating to customers in the new business normal will have multiple points of contact between the supplier and the customer. Sales management will administer the relationship as an "our task" versus a "my task." Sales will be the master communicator and facilitator of the multiple touch points. Marketing will position the solution set against customer problem statements. The supplier will open ways for the customer to access and experience the full range of its capabilities and service.

"If you are perceived as a strategic resource, you are involved in mission-critical applications or functions and engaged in mutually strategic activities. Working at the executive level in activities such as joint strategic planning, you and your customers are helping, on a company-to-company basis, to advance each other's businesses." —Mark Shonka, Dan Kosch (*Beyond Selling Value.* [Chicago: Dearborn Trade Publishing, 2002])

Intellectual property is both disclosed and undisclosed. It is both internally developed and externally purchased. In the new business normal, intellectual property becomes so important it is organized as a profit center for management visibility. It must be relentlessly pursued, enhanced, and vigorously defended. Internal development is behind closed doors, kept there as needed and disclosed to only those with a need to know. Succinctly stated: if it is complex and based on know-how, hide it. If it is straightforward but enforceable, patent it. Intellectual property enables companies to build barriers to entry, cement customer relationships, build market space, and provide margin—all sustainable advantages in any normal.

The future role of innovation and intellectual property is not lost on national policy makers. Alan Greenspan, the chairman of the Federal Reserve, was asked what the "end game" is of offshoring jobs and outsourcing manufacturing from the U.S. economy. He replied that U.S. companies will become more conceptual and development-directed as manufacturing activities migrate to lower-cost global producers. Greenspan continued that U.S. businesses need to move up to the next level in the chain of value creation by being more innovative.

What's changed is that three billion people have been added to the global economic capitalist infrastructure from India, China, and Russia in the past five years. These people entered the free-market world at greatly lower wage scales, some with good educations and most with a healthy regard for hard work. Companies in the United States are tapping these new resources by training offshore workers and outsourcing manufacturing as a strategic measure to control costs. They recognize the growing difficulty of trying to create a competitive edge through production facilities alone. They have little option but to seek cost parity, or below, in a free-for-all global market.

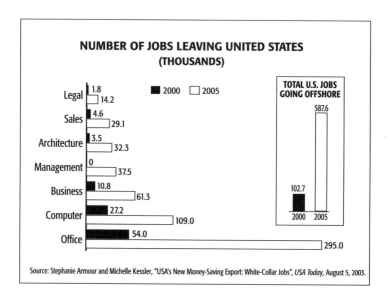

NUMBER OF JOBS LEAVING UNITED STATES (THOUSANDS)

	2000	2005
Legal	1.8	14.2
Sales	4.6	29.1
Architecture	3.5	32.3
Management	0	37.5
Business	10.8	61.3
Computer	27.2	109.0
Office	54.0	295.0

TOTAL U.S. JOBS GOING OFFSHORE

2000	2005
102.7	587.6

Source: Stephanie Armour and Michelle Kessler, "USA's New Money-Saving Export: White-Collar Jobs", *USA Today*, August 5, 2003.

When reading Greenspan, I am reminded of what each of the last three CEOs of Intel all espoused. It is a simple three-word proclamation: "Invest or die." They all acted in succession on the belief that a company secures a position in the future only by investing, by creating something new, and by continually raising the bar on competition through development. In the minds of these executives, Greenspan's "moving up the chain of value creation" would resonate well.

Financial analysts will need to develop new business valuation models that measure ratios and growth rates of intangible assets. Commercial success, in the new business normal, will relate more to how effectively a company leverages and grows its intangible assets than to how many buildings and machines it owns. Book value as a measure of a company's basic worth is dead.

Most intangible assets of a company are now buried in consolidated financial statements or appear in brief detail as notes to the financial statement. Wall Street is still mired in formula analyses based mostly on tangible assets. The real corporate sinew of the new business normal involves the intangibles of patents, trademarks, copyright, and know-how retention. It involves creating brand recognition, proprietary software, and knowledge-management systems. It involves building "virtual" companies around the world through partnership and joint-development affiliations. It involves the unassailability of customer relationships. It involves below-spot market supply agreements and being a leader in setting industry standards. These are the key competitive differentiators in the new business normal.

The paradigm shift of the new business normal is to put more of a company's IQ on innovation and less on cost cutting and efficiency. A company could become the most efficient producer of CRT monitors, mechanical carburetors, wool flannel sports uniforms, or leaded gasoline, but nobody is going to notice (somewhat akin to being the best-looking horse on the way to the glue factory).

A company in the semiconductor industry that provides a textbook-perfect organizational model for innovation and operational balance is LSI Logic. LSI is a semiconductor manufacturer with $2 billion in annual sales. In reading their 2003 annual report, several organizational features that squarely position the company for both innovation and operating efficiency become apparent.

LSI's chip manufacturing is parceled among internal and external (custom) sources. The internal source is one state-of-the-art manufacturing facility in Oregon where the majority of the company's volume is produced. The company outsources its remaining production to custom manufacturers in Taiwan, Malaysia, and China. In operations of final assembly and test, all sources are external. The company uses seven independent contractors throughout Asia for this lower value-add work. The importance they put on innovation is unmistakable. LSI operates wholly owned R&D facilities in no less than 13 locations around the world. They obviously not only believe in innovation but also evidence the winning notion that innovation must also be market driven.

Often taken for granted by senior management is the intangible value that supply chain assets can deliver. "On time anywhere" is more than a catch phrase. In the new business normal, it is managing an important resource and part of the ante required for doing business beyond local boundaries. The words of Michael Dell, "He who has the best supply chain wins," aptly describe the leverage of supply chain assets. Just-in-time inventory management policies of customers are widespread. Producers are moving more and more to "mass customization" in manufacturing. Both policies put a premium on supply chain performance. The responsibility for inventory has shifted to suppliers. In concept and design, a supply chain spans the conversion of raw materials to the end-use experience. In evaluating a supply chain strategy, think through all the steps between competitive analysis and postsale support. "Around the corner, around the world" is a real-life model of a supply chain in the new business normal.

Virtual is virtuous in the new normal.

FOUR

Leadership

Excellence deserves a blank check

"To build a car, we have to build people."
— Hiroshi Okuda, chairman of Toyota

"Leadership is harnessing the intellectual and emotional energy of people by influencing their behavior through values-based frameworks such that performance becomes the residual."
—Michael W. Wright

"Leaders are persons who by word and/or personal example, markedly influence *the behaviors*, thoughts, and/or feelings of a significant number of their fellow human beings."

—Howard Gardner, professor of education, Harvard Graduate School of Education; adjunct professor of neurology, Boston University School of Medicine. (*Leading Minds: An Anatomy of Leadership [New York: Basic Books]*)

Old Normal	New Normal
Vision	**Leadership**
In the age of Biz Dev, PowerPoint was confused with "vision," and exit strategies were mistaken for actual strategies. The urgency was around marketing communications rather than creating real value. Leadership was more about looking good on CNBC than in-the-trenches management.	Now there's a premium on a management team willing to commit for the long term. Serial entrepreneurs from the boom are like World War I generals adjusting to World War II conditions. Success has less to do with looking good than with crafting change-the-world (or at least improve-the-world) ideas and executing them every day.

Source: Polly LaBarre (*Fast Company* magazine, "Welcome to the First year of the rest of our lives." May 2003) Quoting Roger McNamee

Executive leaders make decisions about the future where the outcome is uncertain. This differs from managers, who respond to the direction set by executive leaders through aligning the business functions or business units they manage to those decisions. Executives and managers differ from administrators, who are charged with carrying out the policies and regulations that executives or managers set forth. In the new business normal, challenges to executive leadership start with inklings about future opportunities. The decision-making process varies with the individual, but it inexorably comes back to the simple phenomenon that the difference between a threat and an opportunity is the time horizon in which it is recognized. Leadership is therefore really about the future.

In past years, executive leaders have gotten by with short-horizon profit creation and higher stock prices. Positioning the company for excellence in the new business normal is a much taller order. The leadership metrics for the new business normal are greater in number and harder to perform. They can't be manipulated through accounting and fiscal decisions but must meet the more substantive standards of creating a sustainable company. These standards for leadership excellence are the tenets of this book: strategic customer relationships, technological health, market position, global culture, process disciplines, constant innovation, and first-rate systems for informational flow and knowledge management. Through the prism of the new busi-

---

4Cs OF LEADERSHIP IN THE NEW BUSINESS NORMAL

Competence
Character
Commitment
Chemistry

Source: Dr. Paul L. H. Olson, Sterling Commerce, Inc.

---

ness normal, the benefits afforded short-term financial performance will seem like entitlement without commensurate contribution.

Leadership in the new business normal must contend with unpredictable asset life. What works one minute may become obsolete the next. In the global economy, misplaced capacity is more of a challenge than overcapacity. The useful life of an asset in one geographic region may be much different from that in another. The useful life of a specific technology may diminish at a rate greater than when it was developed.

Workforce skills require continual renewal by everyone in the organization. Skill renewal must be extensive and constant, modeled by the management team. In the new business normal, competitive advantage revolves around highly skilled people able to share information quickly and effectively. To compete in a global economy, a company has to break down and augment the insularity of an individual's experience. Leaders must invest their time and company resources to expose employees to new ways of thinking, outside expertise, and international experiences. This costs money, and the outcome is uncertain. Not doing it will be costlier to the individual and to the company in the new business normal's supercharged competitive business environment.

Markets can and do disappear overnight. The fifteen minutes of fame that pet rocks enjoyed is a precursor of today's blitz of tech-driven product offerings. Unless the customer experience fills a life-sustaining need, the odds are low that the product will have sustainability beyond its initial appeal. Conversely, markets are created overnight, and leaders must be alert to subtle but fast-moving changes in the trends and direction of market dynamics. The speed at which a leader can muster his or her organization to react to a business opportunity will be the measure of his or her competence.

Versatility and flexibility are far more valuable leadership characteristics than specialization. Specialization has gone to a degree of knowledge depth that requires the specialist to be fully dedicated to his or her specialty. Dedication to a specialty has become a lifetime commitment, making it difficult for the specialist to acquire broader cross-functional experience.

A prized capability of leaders in the new business normal will be their enormous appetite for learning. They will need a willingness to manifest flexibility in the face of constant change. The rate of change will shorten term limits of office for all future executives.

A leader's ability to realize something meaningful from each experience (win or lose) and carry that learning forward will be the hallmark of his or her mettle as a leader. (This gets pretty close to a definition of maturity.) The constant shift in battlegrounds, where failures are not due to personal capabilities but are the result of events, requires resilience and perseverance by those who lead.

The new business normal is one of shifting leadership paradigms. Paradigm is overused and, at the same time, is often misunderstood. True paradigm shifts are sea changes. Changing universally held concepts to exact opposites is a sea change. When the concept of the world changed to round rather than flat or when China changed from a controlled economy to a market economy, the term "paradigm shift"

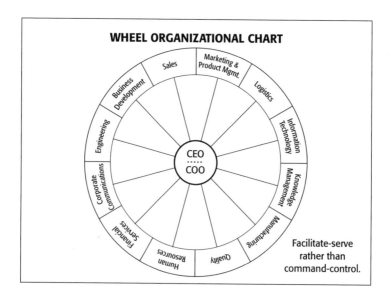

WHEEL ORGANIZATIONAL CHART

Sales · Marketing & Product Mgmt. · Business Development · Logistics · Engineering · Information Technology · Corporate Communications · CEO / COO · Knowledge Management · Financial Services · Manufacturing · Human Resources · Quality

Facilitate-serve rather than command-control.

was deserved. That is the magnitude of leadership change taking place and is why the new business normal is one of shifting leadership paradigms.

Leadership paradigms are shifting from styles of command and control to those of serve and facilitate, from charismatic autocrat to team builder and player. To be sure, a command-and-control style can work well for smaller organizations with simplicity of purpose and mission, limited product innovation, and very mature markets. In that case, the leader's reputation and customer friendships may be the company's divine assets. Charismatic leaders have turned companies around by the sheer force of their personalities and undeterred will. Lee Iococca at Chrysler and Steve Jobs at Apple are perfect examples. But these were desperate situations at the time, with survival being the sole mission. In the new business normal, leaders cannot be one-man bands, nor can they successfully leverage limited experience and narrow exposure. The challenges are multiple and complex. New business normal leaders must be able to motivate and manage large global organizations, create clear mission and purpose out of complexity, operate successfully in a variety of cultures, deal with rapidly changing competitive landscapes, make huge bets on uncertain outcomes, commercialize experimental technologies, and deal with markets that must be expanded to survive.

"My grandfather once told me that there were two kinds of people: those who do the work and those who take the credit. He told me to try to be in the first group; there was much less competition." —Indira Gandhi

Leaders in the new business normal cannot be everywhere at the same time, nor can they have the depth and precision of knowledge of the specialists who work for them. They must be able to motivate others to apply their talents toward corporate goals. In consensus building, leaders need to quickly grasp the salient and shed the amorphous. In effect, the ability to organize meaningful information through encouraging best-effort participation of others defines the role of a facilitator. The facilitator-leader has to know what he or she wants and where he or she is striving to go and must be able to recognize relevancy when at hand. The limited time frame for capturing essential inputs from others will demand that a leader be both insightful and empathetic. The evidence of insight and empathy occurs most often in those who serve others.

Serving Leaders:

- <u>Run to great purpose</u> by holding out in front of their team, business, or community a "reason why" that is so big that it requires and motivates everybody's very best effort.
- <u>Upend the pyramid</u> of conventional management thinking. They put themselves at the bottom of the pyramid and unleash the energy, excitement, and talents of the team, the business, and the community.
- <u>Raise the bar</u> of expectation by being highly selective in the choice of team leaders and by establishing high standards of performance. These actions build a culture of performance throughout the team, business, or community.
- <u>Blaze the trail</u> by teaching Serving Leader principles and practices and by removing obstacles to performance. These actions multiply the Serving Leader's impact by educating and activating tier after tier of leadership.
- <u>Build on strength</u> by arranging each person in the team, the business, and the community to contribute what they're very best at. This improves everyone's performance, and solidifies teams by aligning the strengths of many people.

Source: Ken Jennings and John Stahl-Wert. *The Serving Leader.* San Francisco: Berrett-Koehler, 2003

The servant leader is the most desirable profile for navigating the new business normal. What can be said about the serving leader?

"The servant leader is servant first. It begins with the natural feeling that one wants to serve. Then conscious choice brings one to aspire to lead. The best test is: Do those served grow as persons; do they, while being served, become healthier, wiser, freer, more autonomous, more likely themselves to become servants?"

—Robert K. Greenleaf, circa 1970

Throughout history, those who have served humanity are given more reverence than those who commanded and controlled humanity. Witness the respect that people pay, generation after generation, when entering a place of worship, whereas the power and fear of past royal dynasties today are viewed in caricature.

The very natural act of serving others has been diminished during the last century. The hectic pace of the new business normal lends itself to devaluing the human condition. The most natural response is to push back and off-load the pressure. Technology has eliminated much that is repetitive and mindless. It has provided access to vast informational sources, but the sheer pace and reach of technology have confounded much of what is natural. The leader's ability to recognize and empathize with the high demand levels on people's time and energy and somehow motivate and inspire individual behaviors can only come through the eyes of one who serves.

The need for noise reduction in the new business normal requires time for quiet. Reflection is a critical element in the development of alignment between emotions and thought. Reflection goes back to self-alignment toward what is to be done and how it is to be accomplished. Reflection eliminates the clamor. Think of it like a prelude to course correction or final flight check before flying an airplane.

> "At the deepest level, your soul holds the ultimate awareness; it is tuned in to what is—the sum total of all input. The Leader's secret is awareness."
> —Deepak Chopra (*The Soul of Leadership*, Kellogg School of Management Executive Program, Oct. 2003)

In the large, complex organizations of the new business normal, you must be able to give yourself time to do your job. You have to parcel time to do those things that only you, as the leader, are charged with doing and that you cannot delegate. The CEO is the overarching architect of the company's future. Although the work of strategic planning is often delegated, the responsibility cannot be separated from top management.

Today, the Sarbanes-Oxley Act of 2002 charges the CEO with final authenticity of the company's financial statements. The CEO now must set the company's moral tone through forthright statements and facing up to shortcomings. The ugliness of excessive pay, questionable accounting, and complacent boards falls into the CEO's lap. Determining policies that set cultural, business, strategic, and operational frameworks cannot be delegated. Abdication or haphazard execution of these leadership responsibilities will be equivalent to a criminal act in the new business normal.

The last time I checked, you cannot facilitate or serve without communicating. While better communications remains at the top of the proverbial all-time list for organizational improvement, the essential fact remains that leaders need to develop an efficient communications pattern. This is not a "right-way/wrong-way" issue, but rather it is a style issue that works for the company. Whatever the style, communications must fall into a consistent and recognizable pattern allowing people to repeatedly and freely engage the leadership of the company.

The days of an institution being the lengthened shadow of one person are coming to an end. Leaders in the new business normal will be acutely aware that they can never individually create, sustain, or maintain success. Leaders must see themselves as part of a team, not "the team" or even "the superstar." Neither can they be just marginally engaged until the spotlights are on. Because of the complexity of the business environment in the new business normal, no individual will have the span, intelligence, or stamina to manage an entire organization. Leaders will build teams whose mind-set resonates with the thought that each person on the team exists to help the others be successful. They will put people into positions where they can succeed.

The battle for executives in the new business normal won't be with weak boards, organizational politics, or a hostile corporate neighborhood. The battle will be against global competitors and will be made all the more difficult with the absence of a winning vision. To win will require a commitment to the concerns of the future, not the moment or the past. It will require a conscious recognition that leaders are competing for the hearts and minds of customers, colleagues, employees, and stakeholders.

Leaders will inspire hope in their winning vision by being at the forefront of the battle. Failure to provide that hope will unravel a company's future by paralyzing individual initiative faster than any competitor's actions. Leaders must think about their actions in the following context: Do they provide motivation and hope? Do they encourage people and establish expectations for a positive outcome, or do they foster discouragement and distrust in management? The blame game has no place in a serving environment.

Leadership of a company in the new business normal has renewed emphasis on good citizenship. Good citizenship is a profitable corporate posture. Violating securities laws, environmental regulations, and human rights statutes is costly and distracting and creates bad publicity. The company's credibility is put at risk, and the brand or promise of the brand gathers tarnish.

Leaders in the new business normal want good corporate citizenship as a willing part of their culture and not something that is forced upon them by regulations, etc. This suggests that a strong values framework, from which managers and employees operate, is a singularly important focus of senior management.

Leaders will seek outside directors and multicultural representation on executive committees in an environment of forthright governance and open points of view.

Governance is more about the soul than spun-up public pronouncements. Governance is derived from the conscious and unconscious attitudes of management and is therefore a reflection of their soul. Money and power are the essence of corporate governance issues. When gained, they do not change what the company is; they only unmask its true identity.

Leaders are like eyes—a window into the soul of the corporation. In the new business normal, ocular examinations will be frequent.

Legacy is a key focus of leaders in the new business normal. Legacy is not a story about the past but a condition from which the future has the greatest chance of expanding along positive lines. With a solid legacy, companies in the new business normal can continue to grow in all directions necessary for survival and continue to preserve and enhance their values from a foundation of enabling frameworks. In an ideal world, a worthy legacy will validate the vision and framing of the company by its founders. And it provides hope in the future for all stakeholders, based on the sound selection of succeeding generations of leaders who draw from and continue to shape the company's legacy. In effect, legacy is an employment of people, strategies, resources, and frameworks, both past and present; it should yield a more predictable, though not predestined, future.

Those charged with passing on the leadership legacy will have created a pool of successors, diversified in management and innovative skills but unified in their support of common values. Because the world is accelerating on all fronts, those who would be leaders should be able to identify opportunities faster and take more risks than previous management (i.e., better to act early and have learning opportunities than to act late and end with a mortgaged future).

Executive leaders deal with a pragmatic world that is made of elements disassociated from the world of the rank and file. Investors, analysts, bankers, the press, leaders of other companies, boards, etc., constitute a large part of a senior executive's time and energy focus. At the same time, senior executive leaders must be connected both practically and emotionally to the organization. They must actively promote the vision and hope of the organization on all levels and project that view into all constituencies.

In the new business normal, internal resilience and character will be the measure of a leader. To have that resilience and character will require leaders who possess a great deal of empathy stemming from a substantive desire to serve others—not in a mock humility but through a practical and intentional desire to increase the appreciation of the company's human assets and a definite attachment to the human community. A recurring theme in this book is the importance of human assets in the new business normal. They are, more than at any time in history, key to successfully navigating the new business normal. To appreciate in value, they must be appreciated in fact.

As you go global, you are leaving the first-class cabin seat of the United States and engaging cultures of far lower per capita income and educational levels. This means being in touch with the entire community of spaceship Earth that carries billions of people on it in economy class.

Leaders in the new business normal will not prostitute themselves or their beliefs. In effect, they will not sell out their values and will always be willing to take the harder right course of action. They must have qualities that are stable and inspiring. They will have character (and will most likely be one) and will not necessarily be well appreciated by all.

Leaders in the new business normal will influence the behaviors of others by example. They will be thoughtful and receptive to the energy, insight, and inputs of others. In fact, leaders unable to ignite and sustain the energy of others, relying solely on their own drive, will be like a supernova—bright burn, one big bang, then gone.

New business normal leaders are faced with an overwhelmingly complex task that cannot be handled by the will of one individual. To survive and thrive in the new business normal will take organizations with a team of leaders at the top who are comfortable with the lead changing hands seamlessly between each other as circumstances and environments change.

> Do not be misled: In the new normal, leadership from the soul is not spiritual humility masking intellectual arrogance.

Leaders possessing the mettle and a willingness to face the challenges of the new business normal are rare in number and when found are so valuable they deserve a blank check.

Date _____

Pay TO THE ORDER OF **YOUR NAME HERE** _____

_____ *Dollars*

For **EXCELLENCE** _____   *John Dillion*

FIVE

Streamlining

Faster, leaner, smarter

The economic race is on, and it is global. War colleges today are organized for economic warfare, not just bullet-based war. The race participants have narrowed their organizational focus, rationalized their served markets, redeployed assets, integrated their supply chains, invested in their spinal infrastructure, and optimized their people. These actions are designed to help companies become faster, leaner, and smarter in the new business normal.

Narrowing Organizational Focus

The cry of today is "What are we good at?" In the new business normal, the cry of tomorrow will be "What do we need to be good at?" Narrowing the focus of the organization and its people is a dynamic challenge in the age of information. The more people know, the more they want to be in the know.

The dilemma posed is how best to convert information to action and by whom. An organization's vision is one of the best ways to cut through the myriad of potentials and choices.

That vision must clearly stake out the field of play, and it can be neither ambiguous nor esoteric. People in the new business normal must believe they are running to a great purpose. As I have indicated elsewhere in this book, companies in the new business normal will need to be net contributors to the well-being of planet Earth economically, socially, and environmentally. Building great companies requires committed, engaged people. They become most engaged when they feel a part of a great purpose.

Functions are continuously looked at for their value-creation potential or the cost of creating a capability. Have you ever just stopped a colleague in the hall and asked, "And just what do you do to add value around here?" The answers may surprise you, but in the new business normal, you need to know specifically how you, as an individual and as a company, affect the value proposition to the customer, both directly and indirectly.

In the new business normal, customer primacy is given priority over any self-important administrative imperative. What gets done for the customer is more important than what needs to be done for the individual employee. If you want to get the sense of how successful this experience can be, stay a night at a Ritz-Carlton.

Companies must know their chosen business model and focus on it. Are they an innovator or an imitator? Are they marshalling resources to be the best at design and marketing? Are they building brand? Are they a component or system manufacturer? Do they provide direct services or enlist third parties? Of similar importance is to know the best channels to market for each business model. Without this focus, companies in the new business normal will find themselves managing rapidly expanding chaotic systems of sales and distribution, processes, and policies.

This overarching organizational focus enables alignment to specific objectives without equivocation. Knowing where and how to play well with others on the team leaves little room for debate on the roles and responsibilities needed for execution. Processes can be benchmarked to best of breed, and skill improvement can be accomplished at a faster pace.

Another advantage of organizational focus is the ability to reduce the amount of noise in market data. Knowing who your customer is today is not the same as knowing who you are becoming and who the customer is going to be tomorrow. Knowing when the wells are running dry and the imperative of finding another field will become critical management skills in the speed-based economics of the new business normal.

Rationalization of served markets

Rule of three

"Simply put the Rule of Three states that naturally occurring competitive forces—if allowed to operate without excessive government intervention—will create a consistent structure across nearly all mature markets." —Jagdish Sheth and Rajendra Sisodia. 2002. (*The Rule of Three—Surviving and Thriving in Competitive Markets*, [New York: Free Press, 2002])

In a finite market, three or fewer players will own/control at least 70 percent market share. There are myriad examples of the rule of three as shown in the accompanying charts. Note a subtle message behind the rule-of-three structure: that is, oligopolies are the result of self-organizing economic systems. If there is no other trend you take from this book, remember that one. It is inextricably linked to how you will survive in the new business normal as a part of either the generalist leadership community or the niche community of a given market.

Oligopolies and the narrow bandwidth of consumers are the norm. Well-served markets have been created based on the customer's desire for fewer but more important suppliers.

Name any industry and more likely than not you will find that the three strongest, most efficient companies control 70 to 90 percent of the market. Here are just a few examples:

- McDonald's, Burger King, and Wendy's
- General Mills, Kellogg, and Post
- Nike, Adidas, and Reebok
- American, United, and Delta
- Merck, Johnson & Johnson, and Bristol-Meyers Squibb

Source: Jagdish Sheth and Rajendra Sisodia. *The Rule of Three—Surviving and Thriving in Competitive Markets* (New York: Free Press, 2002)

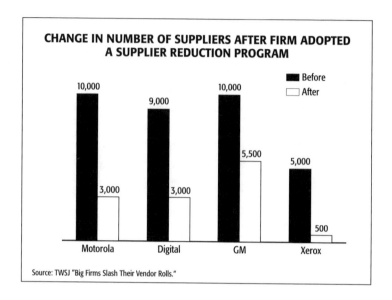

CHANGE IN NUMBER OF SUPPLIERS AFTER FIRM ADOPTED A SUPPLIER REDUCTION PROGRAM

■ Before
□ After

Source: TWSJ "Big Firms Slash Their Vendor Rolls."

Supplier reduction programs have shaped markets, clearly supporting the rule of three.

Here are some competencies and capabilities that you will need to join the top three and remain there:

Adaptability

You must possess a willingness to follow markets to new venues, an adaptability to rapid change in the industry business model, and a clear understanding of the inexorable trends in market preferences and needs. For example, Applied Materials has a process center that virtually duplicates the facilities of its customers.

Contribution margin

Keep a focus on contribution margin by customer as a key metric in the new business normal. It measures the depth, persistence, and satisfaction level of the customer relationship. Making wholesale changes in customer definition and product/service offerings will require extreme flexibility in the structure of organizations. And rationalizing to the fickleness of markets will create entirely new challenges as preferences change faster than the seasons.

Pick winning customers

This will be just as important as picking markets. Which customers in your served markets will be part of the top three? Which ones will be niche players? Which ones won't survive? Which are the innovators, and which are the imitators? The rule of three applies upstream as well as downstream.

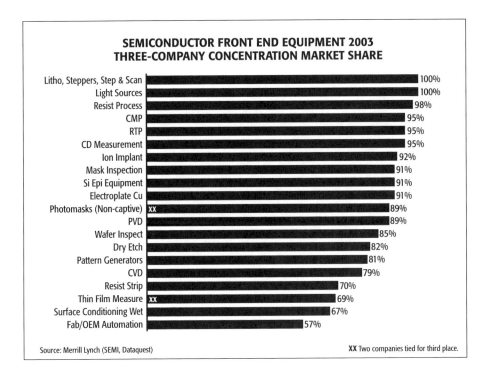

SEMICONDUCTOR FRONT END EQUIPMENT 2003
THREE-COMPANY CONCENTRATION MARKET SHARE

Litho, Steppers, Step & Scan	100%
Light Sources	100%
Resist Process	98%
CMP	95%
RTP	95%
CD Measurement	95%
Ion Implant	92%
Mask Inspection	91%
Si Epi Equipment	91%
Electroplate Cu	91%
Photomasks (Non-captive) XX	89%
PVD	89%
Wafer Inspect	85%
Dry Etch	82%
Pattern Generators	81%
CVD	79%
Resist Strip	70%
Thin Film Measure XX	69%
Surface Conditioning Wet	67%
Fab/OEM Automation	57%

Source: Merrill Lynch (SEMI, Dataquest)   **XX** Two companies tied for third place.

Redeployment of Assets

As stated in an earlier chapter, the challenge of the new business normal is not necessarily overcapacity but misplaced capacity. The underlying asset deployment strategy of a company must be highly flexible and mobile. Capabilities that are exercisable across multiple markets and succeeding technical generations will be prized in the new business normal. And platforms that can add length of life and breadth of application will be <u>highly</u> prized!

However, the political unpopularity of following the customer will make redeployment decisions difficult, if not impossible. The use of offshoring policies in support of more efficient operations has met with political resistance versus a focus on how best to raise the performance bar at home. While a convenient pawn politically, the issues raised are secondary. In the new business normal, global competition is across all walks of life, not just low-cost labor.

Rationalization decisions will be faced on a daily basis:

In-house or outsource?
New versus used versus leased?
Can all production sites be centers of excellence?
Can custom and volume production be done at the same site?
Can we carry only the amount of assets needed to deliver the brand promise?

And there will be new ways to extract more value from underutilized and misplaced assets. For example, transferring fully depreciated assets to JVs not only to create a capital gain but also to realize additional revenues as those assets are shared in different applications from those of the original owners.

And government policies will play an important role in determining rationalization strategies. Depreciation schedules, property and income tax rates, R&D and investment tax credits, and currency exchange rates are real factors for manufacturers trying to offset lower labor cost competition. Government policies have measurably changed market dynamics, and their influence in the new economic wars of the new business normal cannot be overstated.

Physical assets, which are at the core of an industrial society, are expendable in the new business normal. They were once the hallmark of a company's fundamental value. Not anymore—whoever owns the databases wins. As stated in a previous chapter, intangible assets, born of innovation, are the new competitive differentiators. New multi-billion-dollar businesses have been created in the new business normal with few traditional fixed assets. Companies will invest more in business assets and less in real estate assets.

Supply chain integration: Streamlining with leverage

Suppliers must have the mindset of codestiny partners or face a dwindling customer base. A paradigm shift is needed in the relationship of companies tied together in common economic pursuit. Relationships between suppliers and customers and among suppliers themselves need to be rationalized around competence and synergistic models. The interactions between companies that have a mutual stake in the economic well-being of a market must have a unified goal. The companies must hang together out of necessity or be hanged individually out of ignorance.

If a supplier is between the manufacturer and the end user, the supplier must have an economic value or a time reduction feature or expect to be circumvented. If you are not an enabler of speed to market, higher performance, and/or lower costs to the end customer, you are dead.

In the new business normal, more companies will be managing their customers' inventories. Companies will be sharing assets across multiple customers. They will also provide point-of-use quality and invoicing. "Just in time" will mean delivery of the experience at the right time, not just the product at a specified time. In addition,

---

PROFIT GENERATION BY WORLD TOP 100 COMPANIES

World profit $920b

....

Top 100 global companies generated $485b in profits

....

$298b (61%) generated by 56 U.S. companies

....

$74b (15%) generated by 17 U.S. companies in electronics industry

....

Electronics includes: semiconductor, telecommunications, software, hardware and tech related services.

Source: *Forbes,* February 2004.

more emphasis will be placed on value-add engineering. Cost containment will not be accepted; it must be cost reduction. Margin erosion as a result of the proverbial price learning curve will not abate. But in the new business normal, margin is enhanced by adding performance benefits at the same price points. Let value engineering determine performance benefits while keeping your focus on both cost reduction and feature enhancement.

The cost of participation in end markets will only go up in the new business normal. The concentration of wealth is so disproportionate in most markets that even maintaining a position will require creative cooperation among suppliers.

Cooperation

Cooperation will take the form of everything from joint marketing to margin sharing programs. The benefits of cooperation will not only spread risk through shared assets but also will provide new product development acceleration.

Processes

Streamlining in the new business normal encompasses the concept of seamless coordination of systems and processes. This means not only that advanced IT and KM practices be in place and fully exercisable across your organization but also that they work well with systems of others anywhere in the world.

Rationalization

As rationalization accelerates, it will impact both upstream and downstream. There will be fewer but more important suppliers almost by definition. As oligopolies persist and become more encompassing, the supply chain must develop equally larger capabilities of both scope and scale. In order to prevent a complete return to a feudal system, suppliers must integrate proprietary and exclusive know-how for mutual margin protection. Having a 50-percent margin with a customer who owns greater than 50 percent of the end market will be preferred to having a 20-percent margin and serving all of the market.

In the new business normal, expectations will be a moving target. Suppliers "around the corner, around the world" will be more than a catch phrase.

Optimizing the individual to streamline the organization

The return on training can be measured in minutes. No other activity impacts an organization more than training. The how and why are often the most overlooked areas in the development of people. In the new business normal, with so much emphasis on systems and knowledge, having a workforce that is functionally illiterate will be a limiting factor on performance. With scholastic proficiency scores of today's high school graduates sinking, this remains a real challenge in the new business normal and one that cannot be overlooked. This extends to the professional ranks as well, as we continue to mistakenly assume that certain skill sets are imbedded as a result of degree achievement.

While we have heard it all before, continuous learners in the new business normal will mark the start of the next wave of Darwinian selection. Learning, learning, learning is the only mantra that will count. In my career, I have focused on getting rid of the dumb jobs. The repetitive, mind-numbing, assembly line-like jobs are a sure way to lose quality in the product and foster disengagement of the work force. Automate the repetitive whenever and wherever possible, but remember, in the new business normal, millions of low-cost hands can effectively compete with automation. This challenge of the new business normal begs for a low-cost, high-tech mechanization solution.

The training of people is going to be at a higher level. Knowledge training will supplant operational skills training. Training in the use of IT systems, leadership, problem solving, and solutions packaging will all begin to take equal weighting with functional skills. Account management and performance contracting will supplant direct product sales, requiring the training and retraining of many a sales force.

Language and cultural knowledge will be a necessity to interact with global economics. The Internet will remove the need for human interaction on commodity products. The job displacement inherent in that one statement is immeasurable today.

In the new business normal, it all boils down to having the best people in the world assigned to doing the right jobs anywhere in the world.

Spinal Infrastructure™ Model

Streamlining in the new business normal cannot be confused with chainsaw-cutting your way to momentary profitability. The risk of permanent impairment or mortal wounds is too high. An analogous look at reducing the size of an organization as it streamlines is to view it as a vertebrate organism. If one thinks of an organization as an organism versus a mechanical structure, an analogy can be drawn that places the functional stability of the organization in the hands of a very few key positions and people. As organisms become more sophisticated, their nervous systems become ever more complex and ever more vulnerable. Adaptive design work has gone into the evolution of protective structures to support and protect these systems. Organisms have various defense mechanisms that allow much of the nonsystem parts to be shed, sacrificed, or eliminated in order to assure the system remains intact.

Today, humans in the developed world can receive transplanted lungs and hearts, excise parts of their livers, and attach prosthetic limbs. What we cannot survive is damage to the spinal system. One nick in our spinal infrastructure usually, if not mortal, is disruptive to the functionality of our being for a lifetime. Despite the heroics of people like the late Christopher Reeve and the progress his cause produced, damage to our nervous systems remains irreversible and often leads to other debilitating consequences to quality of life and survival rates.

The same is true for complex global organizations today. The systems that allow us to sense the business environment, communicate and coordinate anticipatory actions, and enhance the speed and intelligence of response are vital to the survival of the organization. In the new business normal, the spinal infrastructure of the company must be developed, nurtured, and protected at the expense of other functions as needed.

That surrogate limbs and organs can be outside of the organization is easily seen in the trends toward outsourcing and corporate partnerships. One can begin to envision a company whose only functioning part is a nervous system existing solely on the basis of symbiotic support. The well-being of surrogate systems, in turn, provides the functionality needed to create nourishment for the virtual business biosphere. The risk, of course, is the dependence on life support systems that are mostly outside of the organization's full control.

While the new business normal will tolerate the development of these virtual organizations, they will be vulnerable, and support system failure could be mortal. The organizational role of critical mass will be to keep the corporate Spinal Infrastructure model intact. Streamlined and virtual companies will use other resources to provide functionality as analysis and asset deployment priorities dictate.

Hopefully, the reader can easily identify other examples that this analogy might bring to mind. It is clear that outsourcing, alliances, and joint ventures can be viewed as substitute limbs and organs that allow the organization to shed underutilized or poorly performing functions without risk to the Spinal Infrastructure model of the company. Companies in the new business normal are not hesitating to morph their organizations to protect and build the intangible assets associated with spinal infrastructure discussed in Chapter Three.

As global competition continues to accelerate, organizations will have to determine what their Spinal Infrastructure model will be. I have stated elsewhere that the critical mass of a networked organization in the new business normal is top management, skilled and well-placed human assets, customer relationships, and knowledge management. Theoretically, all other functions can be evaluated for outsourcing. Whatever the body profile, management must not risk the irreversible by misplaced cost cutting (e.g., limb vs. nervous system, bone vs. muscle), neglect of the system, or lack of investment in its development—*maiming and atrophy do occur in organizations.*

In the new business normal, streamlining, going faster, and doing things more cost effectively are givens, but your organization's Spinal Infrastructure cannot be violated.

In the new business normal, the adaptable bird gets the worm.

SIX

Frameworks

Performance is the residual of behaviors

"People are always trying to do the right thing in the world they think they live in."

—Michael W. Wright

Why frameworks?

We often refer to the originators of the constitution as "framers." Documenting the framework of an enterprise in the new business normal is critical to establishing behaviors. They describe both the empowering direction and limitations of actions taken on behalf of the corporation.

A global enterprise is the default structure of the new business normal. You are in a global market, or you don't exist. If performance is requested from multiple regions with individual norms, without a definition of the acceptable means to accomplish the task, behaviors will deviate accordingly.

Assumptions that global locations share the same mores and folkways as those existing at corporate are simply naive at best and dangerously ungrounded at worst.

A corporate mantra like "destroy the competition" can lead to rather extreme responses in some cultures and rather anemic ones in others. Without company frameworks, numbers-driven behaviors may indeed deliver performance, but most likely neither the actions taken to achieve results nor the results themselves will be worthy of long-term praise. In the new business normal, to assure that performance comes as a residual of behaviors, respected worldwide frameworks must be created.

In this chapter, the discussion centers on example frameworks currently employed at Entegris, Inc. Each company, however, must find and develop its own frameworks that define what is fundamentally important to it and thereby create behaviors it holds as crucial to performance. A key premise of the new business normal is that performance is the residual of behaviors. Behaviors are driven by business, organizational, cultural, and strategic frameworks that set domains, boundaries, goals, and metrics.

All behavior is contextual and engendered from frameworks that each individual member of an organization recognizes as boundaries for conduct. Framework-related

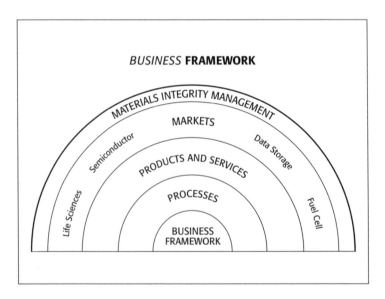

Business framework sets the domain that drives the focus of the business.

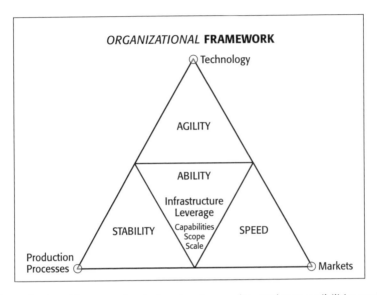

Organizational framework sets the structure, roles, and responsibilities and determines the speed, agility, stability, and ability of the company to grow.

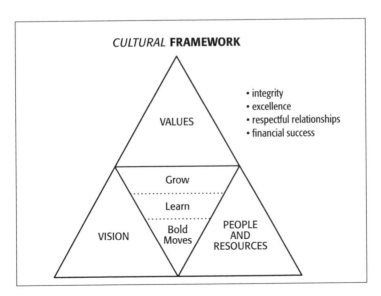

Cultural framework sets the boundaries for internal and external decision making based on values and vision.

SERVING LEADER FRAMEWORK

Five powerful actions that will transform your team, your business and your community

BUILD ON STRENGTH **5**	**Exercise good stewardship of the strengths and qualities of those you lead.** Arrange each person in the team to contribute what they do best to improve everyone's performance and solidify teams by aligning the strengths of many people. *To address your weaknesses, focus on your strengths.*
BLAZE THE TRAIL **4**	**Provide ongoing teaching on the things you expect from your followers.** Teach service leader principles and practices and remove performance obstacles to multiply impact by educating and activating tier after tier of leadership. *Your biggest obstacle is the one that hinders someone else.*
RAISE THE BAR **3**	**Hold high expectations for yourself and others.** Be highly selective in the choice of team leaders and establish high standards of performance to build a culture of high performance. *The best way to "help" is to provide a challenging reach up.*
UPEND THE PYRAMID **2**	**Exercise your power in acts of service to meet the needs of those who follow.** Put yourself at the bottom of the pyramid and unleash the energy, excitement and talents of those you serve. *You're in charge principally to charge others up.*
RUN TO GREAT PURPOSE **1**	**Envision and pursue a great purpose.** Hold out a "reason why" that is so big it requires and motivates everybody's very best effort. *What's most possible results from what's impossible.*

Source: Ken Jennings and Entegris, Inc.

boundaries establish useful limits on responses to internal and external situations that individuals and the corporation confront.

Enron is a high-profile example of a failure to set or follow frameworks that eventually led to the destruction of shareholder value. Its brand and logo became national symbols of business corruption and greed.

Business Framework

In the new business normal, a business framework establishes and/or confirms the domain of the company. Domain creates a set of lookup boundaries in the minds of all constituencies engaged with, influenced by, or employed by the company. This lookup is a set of mental and emotional pictures associated with the company that acts as the basis for interaction. The domain sets boundaries on what offerings and behaviors are acceptable from the company. McDonald's is a good choice for an inexpensive and quick meal experience. However, you would not expect McDonald's to serve a white-tablecloth, special-occasion meal in an intimate atmosphere or develop a clothing line. These experiences are simply not in its domain.

Domain allows customers, investors, and employees to clearly see what the company stands for and the markets it serves. It can also be a predeterminant of a customer's willingness to purchase products or services from the company.

Establishing a domain from a blank piece of paper is ideal. Unfortunately, most companies develop a domain around a specific product or service through default. Sometimes the domain is so clearly and pervasively entrenched that it becomes intractable in the customer's mind, much like actors becoming the character they portray.

Ask yourself whether you would be inclined to purchase anything other than fast food from McDonald's. The answer is probably not. In fact, McDonald's has such an instantaneous lookup for its domain that the company will never become your first-choice stop for nonfood items of any kind.

A business framework is designed to create and maintain domain, and it is the linkage to brand recognition and brand promise worldwide.

At Entegris, we created the broad domain of "materials integrity management" to facilitate expanding the scope of our functionality after EMPAK and Fluoroware merged to form Entegris in 1999. Both companies made products used to enable the manufacture of high-technology products specifically in the data storage and semiconductor industries. EMPAK stands for electronic materials packaging, clearly a specific domain. Fluoroware was built largely from the conversion of fluoropolymers into products useful in the process of making silicon wafers into integrated circuits.

Fluoroware's customers viewed them as the high-tech equivalents of Tupperware products for semiconductor and data storage companies. Given that backdrop, we faced a challenge of creating not only a new brand but also an associated domain that was both connected to the past and broad enough to allow for expansion into new spaces.

It quickly became apparent that we needed to better describe what Entegris provided customers and that it needed to be more than merely a description of a product. Here, another eye-opening trend of the new business normal showed itself. People want to pay for the functionality or experience of a product but not its physical realty. In effect, ownership of the product was secondary to receipt and optimization of its function. Railroads once believed everyone loved the physical reality of depots and trains. They then discovered that few really cared. People wanted only what railroads could do, and when cars, trucks, and airplanes began doing what railroads could do, the railroads were abandoned.

It became obvious at Entegris that customers were paying for the protection and transportation of in-process materials critical to their operations. The yield and throughput of customers' manufacturing processes for silicon wafers, storage media, and semiconductor chips needed to be protected. By our ability to maintain the integrity of our customers' key process materials throughout their production cycle, the focus of our domain has become the assurance of specifications, not features of our product offerings.

In one of those Zen moments we all have from time to time, I had the idea that created a domain exact enough to cover the existing domain of Entegris yet broad enough to grow that domain logically within the conceptual reach of customers, analysts, and employees. For most people, we were a materials management company. But that left little room for differentiation in a large, ill-defined space. Under that definition, one could be a parcel delivery company, an automation company, or a general packaging company. Our current domain of "materials integrity management" has become a defined space, created and owned by Entegris. It clearly describes what functionality our company provides its customers while also being an umbrella for expansion.

MATERIALS INTEGRITY MANAGEMENT
PROTECT AND TRANSPORT

CORE CAPABILITIES   **METRICS**

PRODUCTION PROCESSES

• Polymer conversion	• Aqueous clean/CIP equipment	RONAE
• Advanced packaging design	• Stainless steel	(Return on net
• Fluid sensing and control	• Application labs	assets employed)

TECHNOLOGY

• Materials science	• Global logistics	NPD/ROIC
• Knowledge management (IP/IT)	• Cleaning/contamination control	(New product development/
• Asset leverage		Return on invested capital)

MARKETS

• Branding	• Strategic account management	#1 or #2
• Market strategy		position in market
• Products/Solutions/Services		

CUSTOMERS

• Semiconductor	• Life Sciences	Margin by customer
• Data Storage	• Fuel Cell	

Source: MWW and Entegris, Inc.

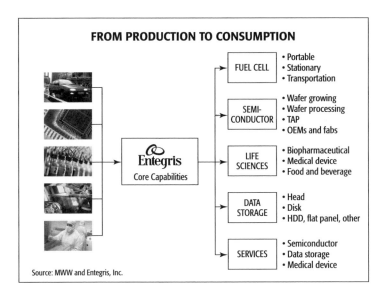

FROM PRODUCTION TO CONSUMPTION

Source: MWW and Entegris, Inc.

Materials integrity management is the business of protecting and transporting critical materials. Most materials that go into the manufacturing of today's technology items need special care when being transported to or within a manufacturing facility.

Today, Entegris is protecting and transporting critical materials that enable companies to successfully bring high technologies to market. By the time this is published, Entegris will begin expanding its domain from protecting and transporting to include purification. Purification vouching will start with assuring specifications for cleanliness. Expansion will occur imperceptibly, but new addressable markets will expand exponentially. Entegris will redefine itself by redefining its domain.

This small but strategically critical move will change the course of the company by adjusting a framework that will influence behaviors inside and outside the company. It will change what we see ourselves doing in the future, how we will leverage resources across markets, and how we will lead our R&D in new but highly coordinated directions.

Business frameworks create rational boundaries for driving behaviors that deal with focus, alignment, and market interaction. They orient the company in a global commercial space and give investors a sense of the sector(s) in which the company participates. More important, they clearly establish a connection between employees and customers.

People engaged in the definition, exploration, and execution of both tactical and strategic activities in the new business normal need to know their business framework. The "where to play" and the "how to play" cannot be left to chance or history. The business framework focuses activities that are related to delivering the brand promise and aligning resources to provide specific functionality to reduce costs and time in the customer's world. We know that knowledge is becoming so vast that companies in the future will have a narrower and rationalized focus. A business framework that rationalizes the company's resources around a well-defined domain will be a necessity, not an option.

Interestingly, a business framework does not define a capability, nor does it automatically imply what core competency or capability will be used to deliver the functionality of the brand promise. In fact, in the new business normal, ownership of the result does not require ownership of the resources necessary to deliver the experience.

For Entegris, our business framework defines us not only by what we are but also by what we are not. No one will confuse Entegris as a conglomerate with disparate operations, serving unrelated industries. Entegris has a well-defined positioning description.

Entegris knows that it cannot survive as just a manufacturing company because of the difficulty of differentiating products solely through manufacture. As stated in other chapters, Entegris must become, like all successful companies in the new business normal, a leader in distribution, customer relations, knowledge management, and innovative product and process development. We characterize global operations at Entegris by direct linkages to customer sites, customer productivity, and customer road maps to assure the relevancy of our domain.

Measuring the success of a business framework in the new business normal

Public recognition of the domain occupied by a company in the new business normal should be celebrated. Singling out a company from the noise that bombards seemingly everyone on the planet, whether buried inside the walls of a company or their homes, is a goal worthy of the effort. Whether from overbooked schedules to voluminous e-mails or from advertising, telemarketing, and sales calls, the end result of the age of the well-served market is a lot of noise. Clamor challenges every marketer in pursuit of mind share.

ENTEGRIS BRAND AWARENESS IN SEMICONDUCTOR INDUSTRY

	AD CAMPAIGN			*OUTSIDE
	2002	2003	2004	AVERAGE
RECOGNITION: Awareness and recall	40%	68%	81%	13
RECALL: Confidence in company and claims	55%	41%	45%	25
DOMAIN: Depth & breadth of predispostion to purchase	80%	72%	80%	38
MESSAGING: Warm and approachable	50%	31%	17%	35
Stable	18%	11%	21%	
Innovative	28%	12%	17%	
AFFINITY:				
Integration into customer sense of self (Fluid)	30%			
Integration into customer sense of self (Wafer)	43%			
Wafer transport		62%	65%	
Fluid transport		39%	40%	
Bulk chemical transport		39%	40%	
Finished wafer, bare or pkg. die transport		39%	55%	
Pressure, flow or level measurement		23%	28%	

Source: Study conducted by *Solid State Technology;* *Data from Marketing Research Council.

At Entegris, a three-year program that focused on a radical departure from the norm in business-to-business advertising created a successful resonance with its primary customer base. As shown above, the results, confirmed with third-party interviews, show the success of the program.

Customer Recall

Brand recognition, or recall of the brand, by itself, falls short as a metric in the new business normal. Distinguishing the brand as a result of frequency of exposure creates familiarity, but familiarity often is non sequitur in building a basis for predisposition to purchase. Well-known sales training consultant and business columnist Jeffrey Gitomer puts it best. He suggests we all should strive to have a brand like Harley Davidson. After all, he says, how many of YOU have your company logo tattooed on the butts of thousands of attractive women and burly bikers? Achieving the goal of customer recall means the company name and logo capture the brand promise in the mind of the customers—or elsewhere. The Harley Davidson brand has become so prominent that the company generates more revenue from ancillary products than it does from the motorcycles themselves.

Reputation

Sustainable success in the new business normal can also be measured by the reputation a company earns in its chosen domain. Is it known as the premier supplier within its domain? Is the basis for that premium held universally or regionally? Does it resonate across the entire customer base, or is it selective within a few customers? And through what medium is that reputation held?

In the new business normal, domain dominance is measured by the unassailable reputation the company has built for a specific functionality that it delivers better than anyone else in the world—not only by fact but also by reputation.

Brand Strength

Brand strength in a world filled with brands is a relatively new measurement. When looking at brand strength, name and domain recognition are the underpinnings, but the ability of the brand to attribute risk onto a competing brand is a compelling measure of its strength. A brand with sufficient strength, as measured by its ability to diminish a competing brand, can be leveraged in the new business normal.

A business framework creates a domain that focuses all stakeholders on the brand promise and sets it apart from competitors. The framework must be broad enough to be flexible yet narrow enough to have clear meaning to the customer. It sets up a clear context for behaviors by the company's employees as well as expectations from its customers and stakeholders. It requires constant focus and reinforcement. It is measurable by recognition, recall, and persistence.

Cultural Framework

A cultural framework sets the boundaries for internal and external decision making by combining a common vision, shared values, and the character and skill sets of human resources available to the organization.

A cultural framework provides purpose for the corporation and for the individual. In the new business normal, corporations must aspire to be net contributors to the global economy and to humanity in general. Without that greater purpose of enabling, enhancing, or effecting positive change, companies lacking it will lose a compelling rationale for being part of the global community.

People need a greater purpose that relates their daily work activities to the outside world. And they must clearly resonate with whatever that purpose purports to be. In the new business normal, expectations for greater productivity, focus, and efficient use of resources demand extra effort. Extra efforts that provide little or no personal satisfaction due to a lack of a greater purpose result in burnout. Said another way, burnout is what you get when you work harder but feel worse about it.

Vision statements are a reflection of the attitude of the organization toward the world. To resonate loudly enough to create a culture (culture is defined herein as what happens when you leave the room), it must be substantive. The best ones can be visualized. Vision statements create attitudes rather than define landscapes. Vision statements, to me, should inspire hope, direction, and, most important, purpose. The shorter the better, as second-language constituents don't do well with long, convoluted platitudes as sources of motivation.

A platitude is an expression of something that is commonly understood but presented as if it were new and important. To achieve resonance, platitudes must be removed from the vision statement. In the new business normal, vision is everything. Without vision, there is no way to connect people to the culture.

Values are a work in progress in a multicultural world. The way to assure that values are indeed shared is to be inclusive in their development. A person with discretionary income has to have patience with a person just trying to survive. Yet there are common human values accessible to any company that can and do resonate with the human community. The values of a company are inextricable from leadership. Leaders set the value tone for promotion, recognition, and reward. Values directly determine everything from who gets rewarded to what is declared on an export document. Values will be challenged in the new business normal by differences in culture and by those who would misuse them for personal gain. Of all the framework elements, values do more to establish a foundation for behaviors than any other. Values set the acceptable and the unacceptable.

Many economic experts suggest that it costs businesses up to 20 percent more to function in underdeveloped countries due to the myriad of delays, corruptions, and other inefficiencies.

CORRUPTION PERCEPTIONS INDEX 2003

COUNTRY RANK	COUNTRY NAME
1	Finland
2	Iceland
3	Denmark
	New Zealand
5	Singapore
6	Sweden
7	Netherlands
8	Australia
	Norway
	Switzerland
...	...
124	Angola
	Azerbaijan
	Cameroon
	Georgia
	Tajikistan
129	Myanmar
	Paraguay
131	Haiti
132	Nigeria
133	Bangladesh

Source: Global Corruption Report 2004, *Transparency International*, 2004, Pluto Press, London, England.

Character and Skill Sets of Human Resources

The multiculturalism of the new business normal means that employees must know what is expected of them and that others must be able to count on it. Vision statements and values help shape those expectations and determine the skill sets required by the organization, but the character of the employees is hardened by the training and experiences they confront when those elements are promoted and enforced.

The role of skills is embodied in the phrase "hold your position." This expression describes the abilities attached to a person's competence and his or her ability to support corporate objectives. The expression requires employees to maintain their competencies to a level that recognizes there is no default safety net provided by others in the new business normal. This puts the burden of personal development squarely on the shoulders of the employee. What prevents that development from becoming entirely self-serving are the adjacent framework boundaries of vision and values.

Skill is an analytical capability coupled with an awareness of all the available tools relevant to the situation. Skill, in the new business normal, will be about what to do within the enormity of the challenges to the business unit or organization. Skill will have less to do with the competence of operating a machine or with using mechanical instruments but more to do with identifying problems, solutions, and opportunity.

The sophistication and educational/training level of employees will be a major determinant of the thought quality of the company. Relevancy and diversification of the experience is more important than its duration. While seasoning in a position is important, it takes a back seat to time as business speed accelerates. Putting people in positions of authority or responsibility because it is "their turn" based on seniority or loyalty could be a disaster.

Understanding technical and operational practices among disparate languages will be an increasing challenge. Language translation of technical information will impair skill development. The challenge is compounded by the fact that English is the language of the Internet and forms the basis for transnational flows of information.

The attitudes that people bring to an organization are set before employment by their ethnic and national culture. To assure that the default settings are not engaged inappropriately or unwittingly, new business normal companies must establish clear expectations of behavior aligned with the vision and values of the company. With rapid changes in the global business environment, where wholesale moves of assets and capabilities will be commonplace, there is the potential for cultural chaos. Without strong cultural frameworks, behaviors run the risk of being divergent, and performance will suffer.

In addition, hiring practices that select people who are predisposed to align with the values of the company will be critical to maintaining the culture. Employees without character will be high risk, and character screening will ultimately determine employability.

In the new business normal stereotyping, xenophobia and cultural fears will persist. Corporate frameworks that combine inspiring visions and fundamental human values with twenty-first-century skill definitions will prevail.

Strategic Frameworks

The fundamental objective of a strategic framework is to set optimal scope, scale, and the parameters of capabilities.

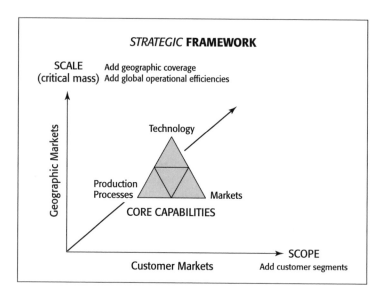

Core capability triangle adapted from Professor Bala V. Balachandran, J. L. Kellogg Distinguished Professor of Accounting and Information Systems

As the cultural framework describes how we do things, the strategic framework describes our aspirations. A strategic framework sets the strategic intent and operational goals of the organization. It provides a filter for M&A and IP development, defines the markets to pursue, and gives a road map of product functionality in those addressed markets.

In the new business normal, replication as strategy (applicable for infinite markets) will give way to morphing in an age of finite and well-served markets. In the new business normal, strategic frameworks will morph the cornerstone elements of the company (capital, technology, production processes, and markets) to align with the achievement of operational goals.

The emphasis or deemphasis given to any particular cornerstone will influence the behaviors of the organization. Strategic frameworks therefore will influence competency and capability development, recruitment and retention, prioritization of goal setting, and the depth and frequency of planning.

However, once set, the strategic framework determines the speed, agility, and ability of the company to grow and prosper under varying conditions.

Choosing the weighting of the elements in a strategic framework determines the biases toward action. In the new business normal, that determination needs to come early and quickly—literally as soon as the need is identified.

In the new business normal, the frameworks you choose irrevocably set the future.

SEVEN

Knowledge Management

It's no longer the haves versus the have nots; it's those who know versus those who don't know

"Knowledge needs context—without context to specify time, place, and relationship with others, it is just data."

—I. Nonaka (Hitotsubashi University,
HAAS School of Business, UC Berkeley)

"Remember, getting the data is administrative, using it is strategic."
—Mark Shonka, Dan Kosch (*Beyond Selling Value,*
[Chicago: Dearborn Trade Publishing, 2002])

"Knowledge is knowing ... or knowing where to find out."
—Alvin Toffler

Knowledge management (KM) is just beginning to take form as a discreet corporate function. At less than 10 years new, most companies do not have even a partially functioning KM system. Managers usually hear KM as "buzz" rather than as a reference to action. If a KM function exists at all, it is often a part of the IT system, or it has been given to the CIO for incubation.

Interpretations of the meaning and value of KM in corporate culture are vague, which explains why KM has had difficulty in gaining traction. Early adopters emphatically maintain that to view KM and IT as interchangeable is misdirected. They concede a tangential relationship but not a synonymous one. By function and purpose, IT relates to KM only as a supporting tool.

This leads to the fundamental observation that the meaning and role of KM in a company should be defined specifically and reinforced often. The definitions used in this chapter are worth reviewing for your own environment. It is important that the definition be crisp and not flow into the realm of IT or to mean specific documents or reports.

KM is a network of processes, people, and technology that combines the databases of IT into business intelligence. Simply put, the KM network turns inputs of data-based information into outputs of intelligence. Information is defined as discreet facts and figures. Knowledge is defined as linked information or a relationship of relevant facts and figures. KM extends into realizing the significance of linked facts and figures. In short, a KM network enables objective decision making from the reservoir of information in the company.

Consider how an actual sales figure compares to budget, a competitor's or last year's. What decisions, good or bad, led to the sales result? KM is using a company's understanding of these linkages to improve products, processes, or customer relationships. In the scale and scope of the new business normal, operating without KM will be like flying a 747 in fog with no instruments. Good luck, or should I say, "Divine assistance desired!"

The importance of KM to the intellectual capital of the organization in the new business normal cannot be understated. In our age of the knowledge worker, job turnover can also be called knowledge turnover. In the new business normal, know-how can walk, and valued information can be lost completely or irretrievably. Chapter Three holds that the most important corporate assets in the new business normal are not the material but the intangible, to which intellectual capital is the wellspring. Intellectual capital is seen as the accumulated knowledge held by employees and corporate units multiplied by the speed and frequency at which this knowledge is shared or transferred throughout the organization. Knowledge is the currency of intellectual capital. How much do you have, and how often is it used (turned)? Does this sound familiar to the care and feeding of some other company assets?

A key repeating theme of this book is the critical strategy of developing systems that allow the company to access, collate, analyze, and apply information on a customer problem or business opportunity anywhere in the world at any time. More important, a company must be able to do it faster than its competition. This hypothesis, developed by Bill Gates in *Business @ the Speed of Thought*, should drive all KM systems development.

In the new business normal, competition is no longer the arena of quality, specification, delivery, or even cost. These factors are becoming part of the "ante" to enter and stay in markets. They will, at best, give parity status, but parity, without KM and its resultant innovation, will be short lived.

Organizing for KM

The demands of the new business normal will make the appointment of chief knowledge officers (CKOs) commonplace in business organizations. CKOs will set up the KM system and establish the rules of corporate knowledge sharing. The CKO will define KM, set its value to the company, and enlist the participation of all employees in the KM system. Senior management, in turn, needs to visibly support the efforts of the CKO through a direct reporting channel and policy statements as to the competitive advantages of KM. Like all activities in a corporation not directly related to making or selling products, without visible senior management support, these activities often languish.

Step aside a second, and ask yourself this question. Has your group, department, or business unit had a knowledge breakthrough recently, and if so, what became of it? The answers may be telling.

The hurdles for developing and using a KM system are usually not the system's hardware or software. Technology represents maybe 10 percent of a KM system. The other 90 percent is business processes and people. The real difficulty of implementation is in providing motivation for employees to share knowledge. The successful business solution prescribed in the new business normal, where success relies on customer experience, requires people from multiple disciplines and cultures to share knowledge readily and extensively. In the past, owning knowledge was associated with power. In the new business normal, contributing knowledge will be recognized as the greater source of power. Swapping advice on a Web bulletin board is easy. The trick is in motivating people to use it.

Most knowledge in the system will be codified (documents) or personally sourced. Dismantling the individual barriers of "not invented here" and "knowledge is power" will remain a daunting task for most organizations. In the new business normal, both are valueless clichés from a bygone era. The former says that knowledge of outsiders is inferior to one's own. The latter says that their own knowledge is part of their personal competitive advantage. The CKO will need to work to change these embedded behaviors. His or her most powerful weapon for modifying human behavior is one of creating a culture of cooperation. Cooperation is at the core of every sustainable social and interdependent society.

However, not all valuable data will be codified and ready for distribution. Some mechanisms should exist to allow highly unstructured information to be shared and searched. I refer to unstructured information as tacit knowledge and believe that part of a successful KM strategy will certainly include ways to distribute tacit knowledge.

An example of this might be "blogs," which is short for "web log." Blogs are unsponsored, personal journals frequently updated and intended for general public consumption. They often reflect the personality and beliefs of the author in an informal conversational style. We see many unstructured blogs on the Internet today. Some of these in the "news" arena are becoming so popular that news organizations see them as a potential threat. In fact, they played an essential role in the outcome of the 2004 U.S. presidential election. They are creating a new channel for information dissemination—mainly unstructured. Blogs in a corporate environment could be an interesting tool to get hard-to-extract data into electronic form.

Some Thoughts on the Framework of the System

We generally have not delved into the "how to" in any chapter. When this has happened, it is in reference to help explain the "what" and "why." There are several well-respected and published authorities on KM to definitively guide the reader's understanding of a KM system and how it can be effectively designed.

KM authorities

Tom Davenport
- Fellow with Accenture Institute for High-Performance Business
- President's Chair in Information Technology and Management at Babson College

- Coauthored *What's the Big Idea?* with Larry Prusak (Boston: Harvard Business School Press)

K. Ichijo
- Professor at IMD Graduate School of International Corporate Strategy Hitotsubashi University in Tokyo
- Authored *Enabling Knowledge Creation: How to Unlock the Mystery of Tacit Knowledge and Release the Power of Innovation* (London: Oxford University Press, 2000)

McKinsey Global Survey on Knowledge Management
- Published by McKinsey & Company

While sincerely deferring to expert authority, I offer some practical thoughts on the framework of a KM system garnered from early-stage experience.

In the new business normal, the more successful companies will filter specific knowledge that is helpful for individuals in their work. The system is designed so that "who receives what" will be without the risk of starving or flooding. In principle, everyone is allowed to have access to every knowledge source either if they ask for it or, with more sensitive information, if they have a need to know. Be willing to accept an 80 percent solution. It will never be possible for everyone in the company to know everything at the same time. Developing a KM system with 100 percent timeliness and simultaneous sourcing is the corporate equivalent of the quest for the Holy Grail.

Keep the basic purpose in mind. The whole idea of a linked IT/KM system is to share and apply knowledge. The linked system should be able to globalize local knowledge as well as distribute and re-create knowledge locally for any specific assignment. Speed is as important as quality.

Also, keep the design simple. Use categories and filters that are familiar terms in your space. Set up categories of information sharing that are broad areas or sites of general interest to encourage sharing across functional lines.

Recruit initial users based on their interest in learning. Include a few high-profile employees. Most people are naturally reluctant to try something new until they see someone else establish "social proof." Get your company's "social stars" to adopt the behaviors, and the rest will likely follow. Encourage diversity by gender, function, and geography. Enlist cheerleaders and those employees with a natural interest. Cite successful applications of the KM system to company goals. Have management or experts randomly monitor employees, who should have info to share, to assess user and nonuser attitudes.

Set up metrics to ascertain what impact KM is having on the performance of your company. Management will need to validate your system with discreet events of progress toward goals that your company values. Is product development faster? Has order generation and fulfillment improved? Do company objectives and values have a more common understanding? Has "global" replaced "foreign" in the company lexicon? If your questions have positive answers, it follows that knowledge creation and application are to be encouraged and employees rewarded through formal programs like Management by Objectives and other individual recognition events.

KM may become a significant revenue source in the new business normal as well as a driver of business decisions. Data have value as a product offering, and knowledge carries a premium.

Once again, a core theme of this book is that the basis of future competition and competitive advantage will be the speed at which a company can access, collate, analyze, and apply information to a customer problem or business opportunity anywhere in the world at any time. This ability to outpace the competition in decision making, based on superior knowledge management, will greatly enlarge the gap between competitors with each successive learning cycle. Stated another way, your decision cycle time will become either your greatest asset or your fundamental weakness.

KM is not just the latest fad among business consultants or the current plaything of software junkies. KM will be a key competitive differentiator in the new business normal. Business models will incorporate KM as an indivisible element. In fact, KM will become one of only three corporate functions that should never be evaluated for outsourcing. The other two are top management and customer relationships. Do not allow any intermediaries or filters between your company and these enabling functions.

> "With everything else dropping out of the competitive equation, knowledge has become the only source of long-run sustainable competitive advantage."
> —Lester Thurow, professor of management and economics, MIT

Being aware of customer needs and responding to them faster, more accurately, and more intimately than competitors are the measures of a strategically employed KM system. In the new business normal, companies will be distinguished and differentiated by how they manage knowledge. For knowledge creation and application to happen in an organized format, senior management must have a vision of its value to the company and visibly sponsor its implementation.

To know or not to know. In the new normal, that is the only question.

EIGHT

Information Technology

IT, the basis of future competition

We all have a pretty good grasp of what IT, or information technology, means and does. IT, in some systematic form, has been used for many years. It originated on the factory floor to monitor and record part production, machine uptime, and similar quantitative data in manufacturing. It soon expanded to include sales data sourced from invoices. A contemporary system, using customized enterprise software, is light years distant from the original formats and has now become a formidable competitive weapon in the new business normal.

Inputs to IT are generally data. Data are numbers and factual bits that are used to describe, measure, and calculate. Organized data are referred to as information. Linked or related information becomes knowledge.

The physical side of IT is a collection of databases, hardware, and programs designed to manage inventories, monitor production, find expertise, manage cash, evaluate sales, codify standards, and a dozen other activities of more or less importance. Databases output information whose value is in proportion to the completeness of the universe it mirrors. Categories of information within databases are expanding as a result of the inclusion of more customer- and market-specific data. The overarching goal of populating databases is to enable the efficient application of company resources to specific opportunities or problems.

The new business normal has elevated the value of an IT system to that of a strategic weapon. IT is now viewed as a key enabler of many of the survival attributes of the new business normal. Speed, instantaneous global reach, on-demand flexibility, the collation and analysis of massive amounts of data, and knowledge-based decision making have become the "ante" features of an IT system in the new business normal. The ability to model the impact of decisions prior to their execution in areas of cost, quality, and delivery is fast becoming an essential element of IT capabilities.

A vision of accessibility for IT in a leading global company in the new business normal could be stated as: create the same capabilities for a diverse team of workers, located anywhere in the world, as they would realize if located at adjacent workstations and cubicles. Knowledge work must transfer around the world as seamlessly as if the communicators were attending the same meeting anywhere in 24 time zones, at any time, seven days a week.

Information about the activities of the enterprise must be available on demand and adapted to a real-time environment. System design must have both the capacity and reliability to elicit employee use and respect. People will use IT systems if they think the information is resident, accessible, and in a form ready for use. System inflexibility can be a restraint as real-time business processes accelerate or shift in the quickening pace of the new business normal. Data integrity is the glue that unites the IT system, requiring objective and rigorous analysis. Said another way, competitive advantage could be lost without it.

Employees in the new business normal will contribute to the IT infrastructure as part of the culture and reward system. Building an effective social climate inviting all workers to interact with the IT system, whenever and wherever, will be the biggest challenge for chief information officers (CIOs) in the new business normal.

CIOs will be selected for their knowledge of systems that apply data versus systems that collect data. The application of data in support of business activities will dramatically increase the scope and scale of IT systems, often leading to augmentation from outsourced data repositories and system grids. Capacity to warehouse data, backup systems, and support enterprise software could fall to subcontractors. Company IT technicians will become more entrenched in the application of information in support of making decisions, setting policy, and defining procedures.

Justifying expenditures for new hardware or software purchases will be determined more on a rationale to support business decision making and less on reasons to upgrade the system per se. In the new business normal, this means the IT system has moved closer to the customer. Therefore, the ideal CIO in the new business normal will be a person with varied line and staff business experience from several corporate functional areas.

The components of an IT system in the new business normal will be specific to functionality. One component will be a local system, or *intranet*, designed for use among company employees. Another component, or subsystem, will be an *extranet*, created for use between the company and its key suppliers and other important outside constituents. Each subsystem will have a unique data profile and method of access. The overall IT system will have broad access to the Internet. Web service providers will continue to enable standards and upgrade the user flexibility of the software infrastructure. (Example: Leading database suppliers are undergoing major rewrites of their core products to accommodate Web services.) Supporting grids of custom-use software, designed for generic system compatibility, will back up the overall IT system on demand. These grids will be augmentative to system functionality and will be used on a when- and as-needed basis. Technology, in this instance, will be available in advance of the trust required to use it.

IT is the central element in the spinal infrastructure of a global company. IT networks will begin to resemble the brain as each intranet and extranet interacts over a larger Internet. The flexibility, quality of thought, and speed of the system will resemble the synapse time between neurons in our brains. The more connections and the healthier the individual neurons, the more active the system will become, and the more actions it will enable.

The Internet has become the common base that allows data exchange across all informational platforms. This ability to integrate data and documents across all platforms is the Internet's strongest and greatest characteristic. Look for data exchange to continue at ever-faster rates among these disparate platforms:

- Mainframes
- Legacy systems
- Obsolete systems
- Macintosh/iMac

- Unix Workstations
- Palm OS
- Linux systems
- Open source software
- DOS and Windows PCs
- Proprietary tapes
- Archives
- Paper-based documents
- Storage area networks (SAN)

The truth is that most companies have IT platforms that are neither proprietary nor unique. Lotus, Microsoft, Oracle, and SAP are available to all. Temporary advantages from hardware and software infrastructure become sustainable only if management is adept at applying the technology and if the company's social climate encourages compatible social behaviors. Competitors can copy and leapfrog even sophisticated IT systems, but they may find company values and the integration of a global system much more daunting.

Companies successful with their IT systems will use formal employee training programs. They won't allow databases to be forums for free-form thinking. The structure of any database should be intuitive. Using only commonly understood key words, topic headings, and acronyms is much preferred. External users (customers, suppliers, consultants, etc.) will be held to the same guidelines as full-time employees. Successful companies in the new business normal will have a company personnel database in the IT network where all employees are listed not only by name and department but also by special expertise.

Slowness in developing a fully robust IT system often emanates from corporate culture. It's quite necessary that IT system training for employees include a respect for the importance of the system in meeting business objectives. Reluctance to use the system is usually not a hardware issue but more likely one of habit and behavior.

The infrastructure of the IT system needs to support the changing composition and business lifestyle of the workforce. In the new business normal, IT will enable virtual work teams among a mobile and dispersed workforce that might include: (1) employees who work from airports and hotel rooms while traveling on business, (2) employees who do matrix work in three or more teams with the same employer, (3) employees who work with people in different time zones, (4) employees who collaborate without meeting others face-to-face, and (5) employees who work with people whose primary national language is different from their own. IT is the only viable mechanism to efficiently and instantaneously connect large numbers of geographically dispersed people and databases.

A robust, global IT system in the new business normal transcends nationality. It allows a "virtual" global network of integrated operations. Communication is in real time via e-mail, instant messenger, or Web videoconferencing. Workers stay in touch by staying plugged in. Operational reports no longer need to wait for an executive to return to the office to be read. An IT system enables tracking and managing in real time.

The CIO of Entegris kindly provided me with a practical description of what would constitute a contemporary IT system that you can check your system against. Does your system exhibit most of the following?

- Globally linked network of data servers
- Global communications infrastructure
- Laptops with common bandwidths and wireless interconnectivity
- Intranet with searching and interacting communication abilities
- Extranet providing interaction with customers, suppliers, consultants, etc.
- Worldwide voice mail system
- Video conferencing and collaboration system coupled with hardware for live online conversation
- Physical meeting spaces at several locations
- Business intelligence tools: real-time dashboards with "what-if" capabilities and search tools that learn
- RFID with new and wider applications: active tags coupled to real-time sensors and communications capabilities
- Outside electrical gridlike connections to augment computing power or e-mail on demand
- Training opportunities for understanding and using the IT system

Be mindful that security issues will potentially slow the adoption rate of most technologies. For example, wireless communication of data has widespread potential but is slow in ramping up applications primarily because of security issues. However, progressive companies in the new business normal are looking beyond security as a protective measure and are instead looking upon it as a key business enabler— one that allows for new solutions that weren't possible or practical in the past. For example, Apple iTunes is revolutionizing the music industry in large part because the company has been able to solve the issue of digital rights management. Other forms of security—encryption, strong authentication, and Web access management—are allowing companies to share information with others in a much safer environment.

IT can make a giant company seem small by creating access to people and services instantly. IT can create parity for small companies, allowing them to compete on product features and unique value propositions without being hobbled by the stereotypes of big or small.

IT is the essential transom for a team-based management approach to business in the new business normal. Direct communications via e-mail, instant messaging, and conferencing create an ease of iteration and exactness across the company that is unsurpassed in problem-solving and decision-making approaches.

On the broadest scale, technology has created the potential for IT systems to redefine a global corporation, one that is timeless and borderless. Terms such as "home country," "headquarters," and "time zones" lose meaning. Key corporate functions will be dispersed around the globe. Financial operations may be centered in one country, product development in another, manufacturing and global supply in a third. Senior executives will locate where their functions reside rather than group together at a headquarters location. Global business models of the new business normal underscore and build upon the comparative economics and strengths of world regions. The depth and duration of customer relationships must be reset for codestiny. IT systems enable and catalyze these fundamental changes. Change is difficult, and leadership will be tested because the challenge over time is to convert everybody to one business culture out of many social cultures and vested interests.

The leverage of IT on the future of world business offers one of the most influential and innovative career opportunities available to young graduates today. Keep the mission and potential in mind, and don't get lost in the details of the hardware and software.

You can't be it without IT.

NINE

New Products

Innovation has become the ante

Most of us think the United States is the best practitioner of entrepreneurship and innovation. Sorry! Korea had no industry at all, and Taiwan was similarly agrarian in the 1950s. In the new business normal, Korea is world class in several industries and the world leader in shipbuilding. Taiwan has gone from preindustrial to being a world leader in high technology. China is so daunting that we have reserved an entire chapter for it. The United States doesn't even win the bronze.

What's changed is that Asian companies in the new business normal see innovation as a process, not a spark of genius. They see change as an opportunity and are willing to abandon the past to create the future. China accepted the cultural shock of a free-market economy as a trade-off for economic growth in the future. Innovation, in these countries, is pursued in an organized, futuristic, and disciplined manner over many years. Theirs is a strategy of growth with perseverance. And for those companies leading innovation, they will create their own view of what the future can be.

In the technical world, we seem to be getting it right. Innovation, in the form of new product introductions, is less from the inspiration of lone pioneers and more from widely organized and coordinated effort. New products in microelectronics are designed and timed to a central industry road map called the International Technology Road Map for Semiconductors. This is a perpetual 15-year outlook on the overall technical aspects of semiconductor manufacturing. For all global industry players, it is the premier forecasting tool and reference document of what technology advances are required and when. Said another way, it is what to meet and beat.

Development costs seem to advance geometrically for each generation of new technology. In the new business normal, one company no longer bears the development cost alone: Going it alone can often result in failure—alone. Partnerships and alliances are created to parcel out development projects and share economic risk. Leading global corporations, who later compete vigorously against each other in the market, will join together with national laboratories, academia, and trade associations to advance technical development and foster overall industry growth. New product development, out of necessity, takes place along the leading edge. Older designs are heavily discounted and become commodities. This cycle repeats over and over again against a backdrop of ever-advancing development costs.

Players in these alliances must have resources and credibility to sustain development activities and meet market windows of opportunity. In the new business normal, small companies will only indirectly become part of key development projects. Their participation will be as a subcontractor or as a recipient of investment funds from one of the large players. Rambus is an example of a small company protégé of a big player. While in a working relationship with Intel, Rambus developed chip architecture that essentially matched the slower clock speed of DRAM (dynamic random access memory) chips to the faster clock speed of Intel's microprocessors, thus enabling fuller functionality of the microprocessor. Major players like Intel invest billions on a private and global level in helping hundreds of small companies design and develop products that support Intel's strategic vision. Big pharmaceutical companies have been doing this for years.

Customer Relationships as a Source of Innovation

Successfully developing new products in most industries comes down to having strong relationships with customers and tapping the knowledge and trust inherent in these relationships. In the new business normal, suppliers compete for the future by forging relationships with leaders and innovators and not with the market's laggards or survivors.

A good illustration of how strategic supplier-customer relations forever changed an industry is described in *The Machine That Changed the World*. This book is a research-based study of how Japanese cars went from being a joke in Western markets in the 1960s to being standards of quality and performance today. The biography of McDonald's is also an illustrative story of the success of extraordinary supplier-customer cooperation. In both cases, suppliers developed and tailored products according to their customers' vision and strategic intent. The supplier became the alter ego of the customer. Open collaboration including the sharing of cost data, employees, and facilities was the norm. Supplier-customer relations in the new business normal are built on an attitude of codestiny, and the Japanese car companies and McDonald's defined the prototype.

The idea of listening to your customers seems so simple, yet how many companies have customers on their new product development team? How many companies have customers on their advisory, executive, or director boards? How many companies try to exploit or manipulate their customers? How many companies are like the manager of a five-star British hotel who said, "I could run a perfect hotel if it weren't for the guests"? I have actually sat in on business planning meetings where the CEO of a Fortune 200 company continually referred to his distributor-customers as "turkeys." I am reminded of a lamenting quote of a manufacturer's rep in Silicon Valley whose first attempt to launch a particle counter as a private label failed because "Prospects wanted to know precisely what it would do for them and why they should buy it." It seems like such a "duh." In the new business normal, innovation and the customer go hand in hand.

Often the customer is the only one able to define a new product or see the application of advanced technology in product form. Because technology is complex, many product innovations can be imagined only by the manufacturer-customer and cannot be foretold by traditional research, focus groups, or routine contact by the supplier. No one called Chrysler and suggested it produce a minivan. Likewise, no focus group saw that semiconductors would enable the development of automatic braking systems. Yet both products are huge successes. In these cases, suppliers didn't drive innovation, but by being in a close, strategic relationship with their customers, they were in a position to participate in its commercial development.

Slow down as you read this. In the new business normal, think "the primacy of the customer." This is not the same as the condescending "the customer is always right." "Primacy of the customer" is about having customers and their markets as your primary source of learning. "The customer is always right" is a solution for settling disputes. If you put anything on your cubicle partition, paneled wall, or computer dust cover, put this: knowledge-based strategic customer relationships are the ultimate competitive weapon.

Mega hit versus incremental change

You've heard the term "businessman's risk." If you apply the logic of this term to new product development, most new product offerings will be a minor extension or variant of what exists. Entegris adding 300 millimeter wafer-handling products to its line of 200 millimeter is an example of line extension. Tide adding a lemon-scented bleach to its detergent lineup is another example of line extension. Extending the brand becomes a little riskier. Nike adding sports clothing and hockey equipment to its line of athletic shoes, Levi Strauss adding dress clothing to its line of jeans, or Starbucks adding music CDs to its coffee products are all examples of brand extensions. Furthest out on the limb are the really new products because they carry the added cost and risk burdens of market development. Examples of successful really new products are Polaroid, nylon polymers, semiconductors, ATMs, and sports drinks. Really new products have an exciting effect in most organizations, and investors often get giddy with a vision of winning the lottery. The truth is, however, that really new products, in the rare event of success, often become profitable for later entrants and not the pioneers.

A company in Redwood City, California, developed a new wristwatch-like product based on technology that allows for the measurement of blood glucose levels without invading the body with needles. The product was unique, and the market potential among those with diabetes was huge and expectant. The launch failed, and the company sought a later entrant to salvage their assets while their shareholders saw their potential payoff morph into penny stock. Yes, xerography was a mega hit for

Xerox, but the Redwood City experience on really new products is much more common.

The speed at which change occurs in the new business normal and the customization inherent in global marketing make the compelling strategy for competing firms one of continuous and incremental innovation. Even in technical fields, new product development usually takes the form of incremental innovation and adaptation over many years. Equipment suppliers to semiconductor manufacturers have continuously improved their products through multiple platforms, automation, custom software, and materials performance while the basic process of manufacturing semiconductors through metal oxide on silicon has remained the same. No company in the world, in any industry, spends more money on development than Microsoft, yet Microsoft's developments are typically line or brand extensions. In fact, an article in the December 2004 issue of *Fast Company* documents Microsoft's innovation dilemma in great detail, pointing to a myriad of challenges, not the least of which is catering to an extremely demanding installed base.

Other factors favor incremental change over the mega hit. Industry standards make mega product and process differentiation more difficult. Regulatory agencies, like the FDA, can prolong the development period and often shape the product's eventual design and functionality. Legislation can create new products or destroy existing ones. Most companies do not have sufficient or varied resources to support the mega hit from "womb to tomb" without outside help somewhere in the value chain. With an increasing turnover of top management in established firms and the emphasis on company short-term financial performance, mega projects can languish, or their risk-reward values can be debated over and over again with each turnover of executive leadership.

In addition, strong stereotypes can curtail mega projects until someone changes the rules. Automobile companies long protested that "safety doesn't sell." Government mandates and Volvo changed the rules to where, today, safety is a major form of model and brand differentiation. Starbucks is another rule changer. They attacked the coffee industry stereotypes of "rich," "strong," "dark," and "full bodied" so successfully that customers look to Starbucks now as a trusted leader in defining pop culture. (Andy Serwer, *Fortune*, "Hot Starbucks to Go," Jan. 26, 2004)

Some mega hits have arisen inadvertently or through an economic necessity to address industry-wide problems. For example, whitish, mutated tobacco leaves were once of little value. Later, they were profitably cut and marketed as "mild" cigarettes, and the tobacco variety was given the name "burley." The overabundance of lower-quality wood species across forestlands and the millions of tons of wood scrap accumulating at mills gave rise to the mega hits of plywood, particleboard, and flakeboard (OSB). In these cases, the motivations did not come from the market. The industry acted in self-preservation.

Hundreds of ideas are needed to begat precious few commercial successes. The man who originated Kentucky Fried Chicken (KFC) first featured pressure-cooked beef in a sit-down restaurant format. During the strong growth years of KFC, he also tried hamburgers, beer-boiled hot dogs, fish and chips, motels and dry cleaning. He kept innovating, but only with fried chicken did he produce a real brand winner. The new business normal requires innovation as life giving, much like humans require water. However, use the high-tech process of systematic, deliberate, and continuous development as your model. If you must, throw the "Hail Mary," but throw it in parallel and not as a substitute for incremental change. Mega hits do happen, but they are rare.

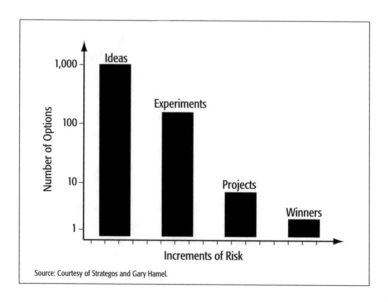

Source: Courtesy of Strategos and Gary Hamel.

Before leaving this subject, there are two approaches to incremental product development, both well established in tech fields, which could be helpful. One approach is to bring a new, but incomplete, product or technology to market, representing about an 80-percent solution. The product launch is targeted on, or partnered with, a customer who is a leading, innovative company in a specific market segment.

Applications engineers or systems integrators from both parties work to perfect the remaining 20-percent solution tailored to the customer's individual expectations. Once accomplished, specifications are set, and final designs are drawn up. The laggards in the market segment usually follow.

Another approach, with some similarity to the one above, is the use of beta sites. Beta sites entail the placement of a prototypical piece of equipment, or component thereof, in a customer's manufacturing space. The equipment is operated in actual production, and its yield, reliability, and overall productivity are measured against performance expectations. Tweaking and modification usually follow until the customer gets the solution and value sets he or she seeks. The term "beta site" is used because it presupposes that the supplier had first (alpha) tested a prototype in his or her own lab before placing it with the customer.

Both the beta site and the 80-percent solution approaches imply continuous innovation. Coincident with purchase, the customer expects to see a timeline of future hardware or software upgrades and a list of options in design and service offerings.

FASTER, FASTER, FASTER

When one brings up the idea of core competencies in a business sense, the usual responses are declarations of high product quality and excellent service. All responses may have some truth, but they miss the point of what really distinguishes one company in an industry or market. Two companies, familiar to all of us, that unquestionably dominate large industries are Federal Express and Intel. What they are best at is quite removed from specific products and services. They distinguish themselves through a competency of speed. In the case of FedEx, it is on-time delivery anywhere. In Intel's case, it is an ability to bring next-generation products to market with ever-increasing frequency. Intel and FedEx established their own view of the future and refused to stop at competitive benchmarking and operational imitation. They developed a core competence of speed and then set out on a strategy of product leadership based on their competency. Speed became their competitive strategy and their way of creating tomorrow. They have forced competitors with traditional approaches to play catch up and make difficult business decisions.

Speed in the new business normal is a measure of time to window of opportunity. It is no longer simply time to market. Speed, in fact, is the essence of the new business normal. Product life cycles are shortening, and new product development times have been cut in half. Markets are so well served that customers expect service in

CUSTOMER PERCEPTION OF VALUE

BENEFIT	CORE COMPETENCY	COMPANY
On time delivery anywhere	Speed/Logistics Mgmt.	FedEx
Untethered communications	Wireless	Motorola
"Pocketable" audio products	Miniaturization	Sony
Performance/Price	Speed/Product Design	Intel

Source: Wright, William & Kelly.

nanoseconds. Learning and knowledge accumulation in new markets are best achieved by launching a rapid succession of product versions. How quickly a company can accumulate knowledge of customer needs and the required product attributes from each version will be their measure of market ownership. The new business normal is a strategy of being first to market and starting the learning process of market needs and acceptance. Waiting for the perfect solution will lose the race.

Speed in product development is often the enabling asset for companies that set annual goals for new product sales as a percent of overall sales. Consumer product companies will set corporate goals for a certain percent of their sales to be represented by new products developed in the previous five years. Speed in the development cycle benefits the company because the product's sales life is extended and its market share is often enlarged. Being an early market entrant seldom causes the product to become obsolete any sooner. Speed also creates visibility. Strategies of speed and newness can create a positive image of the company being a dynamic and innovative leader.

In the new business normal, new product development must be linked with the company's information technology system and its program of knowledge management. A repeated theme of this book is that the basis of future competition will be the speed at which a company can gather, collate, analyze, and apply information to a customer problem or business opportunity. I have often heard it said that the efficiency of a company can be measured by the speed at which information flows. That observation can now be elevated to a statement on survival.

We now live in an invest-or-die economic world. This is the new business normal. The routine and the repetitive will be outsourced to the lowest-cost producer or will be automated. General overcapacity and misplaced capacity in the global supply chain will linger and be recognized facts of the new business normal. Companies will turn more to R&D as their main endeavor. Profit gains will be linked to the increased productivity and value creation their products and services can engender among customers. Revenue and market share gains will be based on innovations in products and services because very few markets are underserved. It is easy to see that windows of opportunity will open and close faster than before and that an organization's speed relative to development and response will be the key feature of its future success.

DNA of Development: The Process and the Team

The scope of this chapter is not to elaborate the techniques and characteristics of professional, large-scale product development or project management formats. Rather, it is to briefly discuss some of the "take-aways" from my own experience in organizing and managing smaller-scale new product programs. Planning a new jetliner for Boeing or a new tank for the Defense Department is simply off the charts.

In my way of thinking, it is important to focus not so much on the tools of development but more on the process and mindset. Most companies have developed their own infrastructure for product development. This infrastructure includes such tools as custom engineering software, financial models, critical-path analysis, IT system access, and review/approval procedures. Some companies go beyond and use analytical and predictive software to define a lifetime cost of ownership of their new product under specific conditions of customer use. Other companies go even further and quantitatively model a customer's production with predictive effects on throughput or yield when incorporating the new product. These software programs are commercially available and have become reliable and objective adjuncts to decision making.

Smith and Reinertsen extensively cover the value of time in the new product development cycle within the book *Developing Products in Half the Time*. They make the point of treating market time as an irreplaceable resource. Once the market window closes, the opportunity is gone. If you enter halfway through the development cycle, you have lessened your potential by the same amount. A market clock starts ticking when the need for the product first becomes apparent, and it doesn't stop until volume shipments begin. In most instances, companies don't begin development

MANAGING NEW PRODUCT DEVELOPMENT IS BALANCING
ACTIVITIES TOWARD FOUR KEY OBJECTIVES

DEVELOPMENT
SPEED
Window of
opportunity

PRODUCT
COST
Gross margin

PRODUCT
PERFORMANCE
Quality, customer
expectations

DEVELOPMENT
COST
ROI

Source: Wright, Williams & Kelly.

Adapted from: Preston G. Smith. *Developing Products in Half the Time: New Rules, New Tools* (New York: John Wiley & Sons, Inc. 1998)

at the time the need first becomes apparent. Usually, development work begins in earnest once a competitor's product emerges. The new business normal makes an imperative of this approach and goes even further by saying that the market clock starts ticking once an inkling is perceived rather than once a need becomes evident.

In the process itself, a top-level executive must be involved in the development at the outset. Give the idea project status by establishing management "handles" such as a budget, an agenda, or staff responsibility. Create a system to keep this project or any project from becoming dormant. At the outset, keep the project moving through incremental accomplishments. Don't launch a mega project where key elements of the proposed product are new to the company. Where competitive products are not available for "reverse engineering," focus on the proposed user benefits and rely on your own engineers to get you there. If the project becomes "hot," organize a task force, run development phases in parallel, and consider using outside consultants or subcontractors. Above all else, keep target customers in the loop.

Another "take-away" is in the scope of the process. Managing a new product development effort is essentially a process of balancing activities toward four key objectives: (1) overall development program cost, (2) the cost to produce the product in manufacturing, (3) the required product performance profile, and (4) the speed at which the development should proceed. The first objective determines ROI, the second gross margin, the third quality, and the fourth time to window of opportunity. In use, there are some variations in definitions, but the mind-set for defining, managing, and making trade-offs among these objectives is the key to eventual profitability. And paramount in your mind-set, understand that the customer is the final arbiter.

The December 2004 issue of *Fast Company*, the same one that documents Microsoft's development woes, also points to W. L. Gore as one of the most innovative companies in the world. The magazine outlines the following keys to Gore's success:

W. L. Gore's new rules of business start with breaking the old rules.

The Power of Small Teams
Gore tries to keep its teams small (and caps even its manufacturing plants at 200 people). That way, everyone can get to know one another and work together with minimal rules, as though they were a task force tackling a crisis.

No Ranks, No Titles, No Bosses
Employees, dubbed "associates," have "sponsors," who serve as mentors, not bosses. Associates decide for themselves what new commitments to take on. Committees evaluate an associate's contribution and decide on compensation. There are no standardized job descriptions or categories: Everyone is supposed to be like an amoeba, taking on a unique shape.

Take the Long View
Gore is shockingly impatient with the status quo but patient about the time—often years, sometimes decades—it takes to develop revolutionary products and bring them to market.

Make Time for Face Time
There's no hierarchical chain of command; anyone in the company can talk to anyone else. Gore discourages memos and prefers in-person communication to e-mail.

Lead by Leading

Associates should spend some of their time—usually around 10 percent—pursuing speculative new ideas. Anyone is free to launch a project and be a leader so long as he or she has the passion and ideas to attract followers. Many of Gore's breakthroughs started with one person acting on his or her own initiative and developed as colleagues helped in their spare time.

Celebrate Failure

Don't stigmatize it. When a project doesn't work out and the team kills it, they celebrate with beer or champagne just as they would if it had been a success. Celebrating a failure encourages risk taking.

A final "take-away" is found in the development team itself. Bring as much firepower to the table as you can. Distinguishing factors of new product development in the new business normal are a time-based mind-set and an open, flexible process. In effect, it's about the people you put on the team.

Product development is not the domain for only design engineers, applications engineers, and process engineers. Financial staff should be team members to track budgets and financial metrics. Salespeople need a presence, not only to speak for the customer but also to provide the perspective of the entire market. Marketing needs to be at the table in order to draft informed new product releases and media promotions as well as to plan trade show participation. IT needs to be involved to assure that the network is accessed and updated. Outside consultants in energy, for example, may perfect the design for maximum efficiency in power consumption. The possibilities go on. In the new business normal, the development team must reflect the facts that knowledge is broadly diffused, the global market is multicultural, and getting a competitive edge is more and more difficult. For technology companies, product development is no longer just a push out from engineering.

Dame Anita Roddick, founder of the Body Shop International, U.K., once said, "I would rather be faced with trying to achieve harmony and goodwill among creative people who are at one another's throats than with trying to squeeze an ounce of innovation or creativity or risk out of a company full of clones."

What's Your Proposition?

We all have experienced the sudden effect of a macro event equaling the benefit of several well-thought-out product launches. Opportunity can knock suddenly and without foresight. Oil shortages sell more fuel-efficient cars. Hurricane warnings sell plywood. Terrorism sells security devices. A financially strapped competitor suddenly wants to cash in and offers an accretive deal.

These things happen. But look at product development in our tough, competitive times without windfalls and without anomalies. What does the new business normal mean in terms of how a company decides what products to develop, and what proposition does the company make with the marketplace?

Start with a clear understanding of the likely profile of your customer base—if it is surviving in the new business normal—and let it be the first screen for development decisions. Companies—your customers—are the ones that, in the new business normal, create and manage knowledge. They automate or outsource the routine or repetitive. They use a supply chain as a competitive weapon. They do not let intermediaries get between themselves and their customers. They use R&D and innovation to create the future. They enter into alliances and partnerships to share economic risk and to gain global access. By definition, then, your product, process, and technology-development programs become the enabling links to growth through strategic customer relationships.

Given that the marketing strategy of a company will direct its product development program, what marketing filters can we use to affirm and guide development proposals?

The new business normal requires you to place your marketing focus on the capital productivity of customers. Make customers more efficient, and make it measurable. Keep your marketing focus on the advanced production processes of your customers, as all displaced technology quickly becomes a commodity. Set a marketing focus to build a continuing presence in Asia where outside incoming investment flows have reached $100 billion annually. Expand your IT and KM systems to include comprehensive intelligence about your customers, your markets, and the multicultural world you compete in.

Finally, what sales propositions and key messages do you use to link the products or technologies you have under development with customers? What resonates today? What are customers looking for and listening to? What will they pay for?

With few exceptions, customers are opting for short-term solutions. They buy if the benefit is traceable and tangible. They buy if there is an economic message, not a message of technology for technology's sake. They buy incrementally. They buy productivity gains. They buy competitive advantages. They buy high returns on assets. They will swap a dollar of capital cost for a dollar of direct cost. They buy road maps of continuous improvement. They buy trust, confidence, and credibility to allay their fears of uncertainty. They buy working relationships. They buy share-the-risk, share-the-reward propositions. They buy codestiny. In the new business normal, you simply must live in the customer's world.

Ante Up!

TEN

China and the Power of Emerging Markets

The game changer for centuries

C hina is the center of world economic attention and for very good reason. You cannot name a multinational corporation that has not been affected by low-cost manufacturing in China or by the lure of selling into China's huge domestic market. China today is not your father's vision of rickshaws, coolie hats, sampans, and fortune cookies. Its transformation and accomplishments have been dazzling. It is a player. The question is to what extent it will disrupt and dominate.

The numbers and statistical trends related to China tell some of the story.

- 22 percent of the world's population
- Fastest-growing economy in the world in past 25 years at a CAGR of 9 percent
- Foreign trade growth in the same period of 15 percent CAGR

- Attracts more direct foreign investment than the United States, exceeding $50 billion annually. That's roughly $1 billion each week.
- Exploding domestic market growth. China now manufactures 75 percent of the world's toys, 58 percent of the clothes, and 29 percent of the mobile phones according to McKinsey Quarterly ("China Today," 2004)

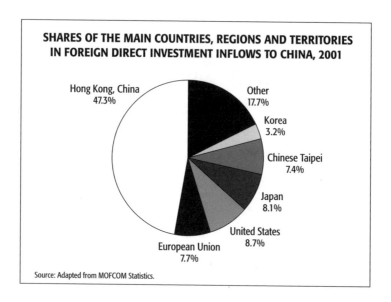

SHARES OF THE MAIN COUNTRIES, REGIONS AND TERRITORIES IN FOREIGN DIRECT INVESTMENT INFLOWS TO CHINA, 2001

Hong Kong, China 47.3%
Other 17.7%
Korea 3.2%
Chinese Taipei 7.4%
Japan 8.1%
United States 8.7%
European Union 7.7%

Source: Adapted from MOFCOM Statistics.

China is the new business normal. Its planned transformation from a controlled economy to a market economy, its gradual easing of foreign investment restrictions, and its approach to WTO qualification show its horizons to be long and its virtue to be perseverance. The Chinese economic orbit is so strong that the country may well be a proxy for the world market because all major players will eventually meet there to defend and hone their competitive positions. China will drive cost and quality parity in all markets it chooses to address.

China's trump card in world markets is abundant cheap labor, creating a decisive competitive weapon for years to come. Almost all international investors see China as the world's workshop, the top location for labor-intensive operations—millions of cheap hands performing repetitive tasks. Low-cost manufacturing has driven explosive rates of expansion in the Chinese economy.

Unrelenting Competition

The new business normal will be one of unrelenting competition. Competing with China is and will continue to be a gargantuan struggle. World commodity prices have risen, yet prices of Chinese-made finished goods have not, creating a painful profit squeeze for off-mainland competitors. Low labor costs will exist for decades because so much of the population is unemployed and so much of the country west of the East Coast is underdeveloped. China will compete on price versus profitability to fill plants and employ people. No company competing with the Chinese infrastructure will gain a sustained competitive advantage. The alternatives of the new business normal are either to eventually produce in China and use the cost advantages of the Chinese infrastructure or to continue to move up the curve of technology and innovation.

There are few Chinese brands today with global stature or recognition. This is about to change, and many Western companies will rue the day a Chinese brand appears in their market. As more Chinese companies take the world stage to establish their brands, there will be design and lower price attributes to their products, along with millions of offshore Chinese, rabidly loyal to the homeland, waiting as a captive market. This cannot be understated.

Haier is likely to become China's first true multinational company. It already has cornered half of the U.S. compact refrigerator market. Its products are routinely found in U.S. motel rooms, suites, and kitchenettes. Other standout Chinese companies taking global aim are Lenovo (computers), TCL (TVs), Bird (mobile phones), Wahaha (beverages), Geely (cars), Tsingtao (beer), and Li-ning (clothing). There are more. China Inc. is about to create a global marketing tsunami with a very simple strategy of selling quality products at low prices. The Chinese call this "selling gold at the price of silver."

How do we know the tsunami is coming? One of the most foretelling trends is the growth of companies that design new semiconductor chips. Approximately 500 of these design centers will exist in China by the year 2005, up from a base of 100 just three years ago. New chip functionality will enable design and performance changes in Chinese-branded products to enhance their global appeal and competitiveness.

The Culture of Government

China's sea level change from a managed economy to a market economy puts the culture of government at center stage for many years to come. Government relations are a high cultural calling. Strong political skills for management have been more important than knowledge of modern business management practices. This condition is an outgrowth of state-owned businesses where intercompany relationships are controlled. More then 300,000 state-run businesses remain in China, of which 70 percent are estimated to be unprofitable. The need for political clout fosters an importance of intermediaries and lobbyists currying favor throughout the varying tiers and quality levels of government.

Governmental relations in China are a sober and detailed undertaking. Commercial law has been almost nonexistent and is arbitrarily enforced. Business does not rank high in China's agrarian culture. The legal system in China is undeveloped, which undermines enforcement of intellectual property rights. Judges usually don't have legal backgrounds. They are typically ex-military or friends of the provincial officials who appoint them.

The Chinese government has identified the electronics industry in China as a "pillar" or mainstay industry (one of six such industries). Pillar industries are enabling industries that are necessary to promote overall national economic development. Enterprises with pillar classification are usually afforded the full benefit of industrial policy instruments and an expediency of action. This is a real jump start and often a guarantee of harmonious and profitable operations.

Start-up and operational costs for foreign firms locating in China can be materially influenced through government relations. Up for grabs in government relations are such assets as free land, subsidized training, tax concessions, low-interest loans, interest-free loans, trade and distribution rights, direct government investment (equity), power and environmental permits, and grants for research and development. Guanxi (personal connections) and zhongjian ren (the intermediary) shape the new business normal of China. Who you know, and how much they are paid, matters.

China and High Tech

China's hierarchical culture is in sharp contrast to the business structures of Western high-tech firms that tend to flatten out organizational models through empowerment, matrix teams, and knowledge. While the Chinese culture seeks order, Western technology businesses are often characterized by "organized or managed chaos."

The Chinese culture of obedience to a "father figure" has created weak middle management that is good at carrying out tasks but uninspired to optimize the business. Middle management is administrative rather than executive. They carry out the decisions of others, opting not to take a position on issues where the outcome is uncertain. Irrespective of ability, Chinese people favor their own family and network. Nepotism is a given.

Unquestionably, the main problem facing high-tech firms wanting to commercialize intellectual property in China is the lack of rights enforcement. Poverty and position drive much cultural behavior. Local officials are slow to promote enforcement because counterfeit production supports the local economy. Motivated by abject poverty, there are few people in the world more adept as small-scale entrepreneurs than the Chinese. The Chinese are predisposed to risk. They love cash, and they love to gamble. The new business normal has the inherent assumption that some piracy will take place. The only alternative is not to participate.

China is using Taiwan as its model to create an internationally competitive semiconductor industry. China has not lost sight of the fact that in the 1970s, Taiwan was a poor agrarian society. One generation later, Taiwan became the dominant custom (foundry) semiconductor manufacturing center in the world and is regarded as among the industry's most efficient manufacturers. Taiwan grew by embracing foreign capital and by offering key inducements for direct investment. Taiwanese nationals, with accumulated experience at Western semiconductor firms, were induced to return to Taiwan to establish new Taiwanese enterprises. Financial assistance was offered to private firms. Flagship industrial parks were organized with infrastructure clusters. Government research institutes were privatized. State control was jettisoned. China, being the ultimate fast follower and copier, has mimicked Taiwan and, in the process, is drawing in record direct foreign investment, technology, and talent. The new business normal of world competition is not only abundant low-cost labor, but it also adds the foreign dimensions of technology, capital, and expertise and supports them with massive government efforts in planning, motivation, and control.

China's future position as a major player in high technology is a foregone conclusion. The fastest-growing segment of the semiconductor industry, in terms of new entrants, is one where a company will design and market chips but farm out their manufacture. These so-called fabless companies have arisen because of the exceptionally high cost to build and equip a new advanced production facility: $2 billion, plus or minus. The makers of custom chips for the "fabless" companies are called foundries, and China's growth model is entirely one of foundries. By the year 2050, China foresees 200 semiconductor facilities in operation or a combined investment of $400 billion at today's cost. How many states in the United States, or countries in the world, have yet to plan even their first?

Get Involved

Nonmilitary events of the magnitude of China's shift from a controlled economy to a market economy, with its vast potential opportunity, happen but a few times in history.

There is peril in seeking profit in this transformation, because all the opportunity exists in a fast-changing, somewhat alien, and high-risk operating environment. But the greater peril is in doing nothing. In essence, China presents two very significant business opportunities: direct access to its huge domestic market and a source for low-cost manufacturing and assembly. To ignore these is to put a first and second mortgage on your future.

It is hard to imagine having done nothing at this late date. Most of the "should we" studies now have their "how do we" sequels. As we stated in the new products chapter, the important thing is to begin the learning process and build knowledge. Contact the U.S. Foreign Service. Work through your industry's trade association. Consult global financial services companies. Attend trade shows. Conduct your next board meeting in China. Invite key suppliers to share their experiences. Price out having something produced in China. Place direct sales people in China. Organize a task force on China and have it report directly to the COO or CEO. The list goes on. The point is to keep going and give your effort high visibility and priority.

By embracing the new business normal, companies will be, or are already, in the pursuit of opportunities in China. They will have already established many of the prized characteristics of companies in the new business normal and of the executives who run them: global vision, cultural assimilation, language fluency, multinational management teams, and competency in IT and KM. The new business normal of the future of the corporation is to innovate and manage the creation but outsource its execution and administration. China was the determining factor of this vision.

Postscript to China: India

China is not the only billion-person country where work gets done for a fraction of the price. Enter India with its smart, educated cadre of English-speaking people eager to work.

India has set up its own orbit in the world economy and has become a player in the new business normal.

According to *Wired* magazine, February 2004, technology companies represent four of the top five U.S. employers in India (GE 17,800, HP 11,000, IBM 6,000, and

Dell 3,800). In this same issue, they predict that the percentage of jobs in IT being sent offshore will accelerate dramatically in the next three to four years. This will be on the order of three to 10 times from their current levels. Most of these jobs will go to India.

India has become a favorite global outsourcing site for call centers, software programming and maintenance, and customer service and support functions. But that is only the start. Coming are skilled Indian knowledge workers, at 10 percent of their U.S. counterpart's salary, performing financial analysis, architectural design, graphic design, clinical research, and other similar routine professional tasks that require computer networks, not physical proximity.

India, aside from its image of poverty, is now ranked in the top 10 countries worldwide in R&D expenditures. India has strategic competitive advantages that China can't match—operations that do not require extensive physical infrastructure and the English fluency of the Indian population.

It could be that nanotechnology—building physical forms atom by atom—will someday change the nature of manufacturing to where it will be economical to produce anything in the United States and thus offset China's infrastructure. It could be that advances in wireless and broadband connectivity will someday mitigate the competitive advantages India possesses in IT. These are stories yet to be written. The prime time of the new business normal is a disruptive and harsh struggle where the aspirations of billions of people are pushing their governments to find ways to join the hierarchy of the developed world.

该是学如何玩麻将的时后!

ELEVEN

Demographics and Debt

The challenges of the double D's

The biggest changes among all those creating the new business normal will come from what I call the Double D's: demographics and debt. These changes are powerful, protracted, and unprecedented. They are not widely observed in the short-term focus of the business community because they are insidious and they develop and play out over a long period of time. The demographics of the new business normal are shaped by the bulge in the composition of the population known as the "baby boomers" and by a deep-seated debate over the desirability of population growth. The successful management of debt is inextricably linked to the very issues of population and economic growth that are creating such profound discomfort and debate.

The most prominent demographic of the new business normal, already in evidence in the United States, western Europe, Japan, and Australia, is the impending retirement of the baby boomer generation. Baby boomers are those born from 1946 to 1964 who number 83 million in the United States alone.

Technically, the year 2006 begins an 18-year period when baby boomers attain the retirement age of 60 at a rate of one every seven seconds. This 18-year workforce exodus will create a dislocation of knowledge, skills, experience, and relationships unprecedented in corporate America. These attributes, for the most part, cannot be inherited or bequeathed. They must be captured, preserved, or replaced. The threat of knowledge depletion from the widespread retirement of a corporation's most senior and experienced workers has given emphasis to knowledge management as a core organizational objective.

Given the choice, boomers want to retire and create another lifestyle. Rutgers University Center for Workforce Development published a survey indicating that 76 percent of baby boomers want(ed) to retire by age 50.

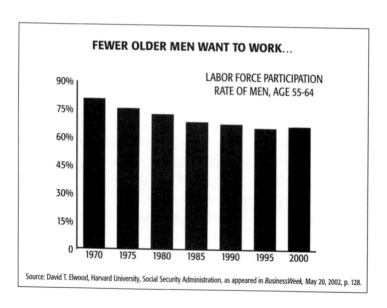

FEWER OLDER MEN WANT TO WORK...

LABOR FORCE PARTICIPATION RATE OF MEN, AGE 55-64

Source: David T. Elwood, Harvard University, Social Security Administration, as appeared in *BusinessWeek*, May 20, 2002, p. 128.

Some larger, older companies will see 40 to 50 percent of their management retire by the end of 2005 (Development Dimensions Inc.). By 2010, the Bureau of Labor Statistics estimates that 60 percent of management will retire from the oil and gas industry. In the same industry, the Society of Petroleum Engineers projects that 44 percent of its petroleum engineers will retire by 2010.

The U.S. General Accounting Office states that by 2005, more than 50 percent of federal employees will be eligible for retirement. This includes 71 percent at the senior executive service level; 58 percent at the highest manager rank, G-15; and 41 percent at the G-14 level.

At the state level, Wisconsin is representative. Almost half of all state and local employees in Wisconsin will become eligible to retire by 2016 according to the Wisconsin State Government Workforce Planning Team.

In the new business normal, two discernible workforces have broadly taken shape: the under-fifties and the over-fifties. When the over-fifties retire, many won't completely stop working. They may actually seek retirement to launch their second career. They will work arm's length, independently or temporarily, but they will usually be related to a corporate structure. They may become dealers, distributors, agents, or franchisees for their former employers. They may consult in their area of business competence and connections. Knowledge workers will eventually become the largest single group of older Americans in the workforce.

Human resource departments will need to develop productivity and motivational metrics for the over-fifties as consultants, part-timers, or temporaries and create a work environment where they can flourish as "professionals" outside of the corporation's hierarchy. Policies covering their access to IT and extranet compatibility will change, as will guidelines for reporting and claims to intellectual property rights.

Above all, corporations will need to capture the knowledge and experience of these aging workers in an organized process. The rate of change in the new business normal can rapidly diminish the value of learned technical knowledge, yet the over-fifties offer networks of access, a sense of verticality, an outside perspective, and the experience of "having done that," which become valuable linkage throughout the company's business framework.

A second profound demographic shaping the new business normal is that of declining birthrates in several developed countries to levels where parents are not reproducing themselves. Most birthrates in European countries now average a frightful low of 1.3 per childbearing woman. The rate in China is 1.8, Japan's rate is 1.4, and the United States is down to 1.8.

Japan's problem is particularly vexing. Its population is already aged. In 25 years, as much as one-half of the adult population will be 65 or older, while its current birthrate has plunged to 1.4 per childbearing woman. Because of these dynamics and the fact that Japan is a homogenous society with tight immigration restrictions, Japan's population is projected to peak at 125 million and then actually decline to 95 million by 2050.

With birthrates lower than reproductive parity in most developed countries, the proportion of the number of young people in the population is shrinking while the number of older people in the adult population is rising sharply. Increasing life expectancy has also swelled the ranks of seniors through advances in health sciences, medical care, and the availability of government-sponsored medical insurance. More life-enhancing benefits are sure to be in our futures as new technologies ramp up in biological, health, and medical science.

What's changed is that the mass market is splitting. It is no longer dominated by pop culture and appearances of the young. Older adults have become commercially and politically relevant. Madison Avenue has pinpointed the over-fifties in the cross-hairs of mass marketing. Years ago, when the baby boomers attained some economic independence, no one over the age of 30 ever appeared in a commercial. Today, it is all about life enhancement of seniors through pharmacology, part-time investment opportunities, and packaged tours that follow the sun. The over-fifties reinforce the key concept of marketing the experience of using a product rather than of promoting ownership of the product itself.

With birthrates declining, some countries will need immigrants to maintain their workforces. Others will look to immigration just to maintain their population base. Neither will be without controversy because immigrants may be needed, but they are not always wanted. Nonetheless, corporations will need to realign for the cultural assimilation and training of their increasingly diverse workforces.

Rising immigration contributes to further splitting and segmentation of the mass market. Entire shopping centers exist in California and elsewhere around ethnic cultures. Media are fragmenting at an accelerating rate as companies seek specific eyeballs and custom products are proliferating into expressions of individual taste. In the United States, immigrants are dispersed geographically, and a large minority integrates mainstream society through marriage with nonimmigrants. Immigrants tend to be young, and first-generation mothers are inclined to have family births above the replacement rate. Superior learning habits and educational values drive many immigrants into knowledge work, providing greater mobility and rising disposable income.

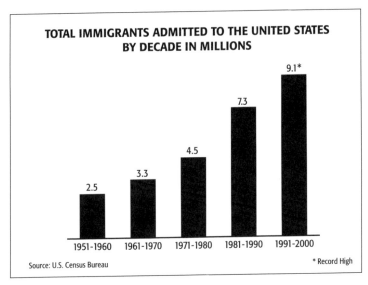

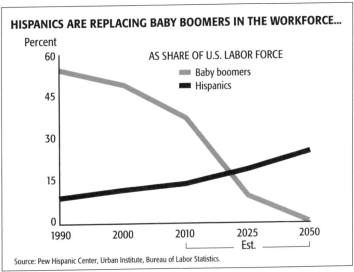

Opportunities for companies to identify and enter these splintered markets and submarkets of ethnicity are growing rapidly. Mass marketing has already given way to mass customization. The demographics of the new business normal will extend mass customization to rifle-shot or micromarketing, from cultural adoption (HMOs) to individual preferences (patient experience).

Looking ahead, there is the prospect that robots with vision and manipulation capabilities will someday reorder immigration patterns. Migrant farm and personal services jobs may give way to automation and lessen both the need for unskilled immigrants and the incentive for them to resettle. Robotics also has the potential to influence the outsourcing of labor from developed to underdeveloped countries. Scientific advances will enable the encroachment of automation on larger and larger areas of paid hand labor. Comparative economics will decide the viability of either.

Debt

The accidental death of John Kennedy, Jr., was a tragic loss of a young and gifted life. The 1,523 people drowning or freezing to death at the sinking of the Titanic is so enormous and remote it becomes a statistic. Similar incomprehensibility applies to debt figures. I understand what owing $450 on my credit card means, but what does a gross public debt of $7.4 trillion mean? What does running a budget deficit at the federal level of $1.2 billion a day mean? Is it of any matter to run a merchandise trade deficit of $55 billion each month? Is it of anyone's concern that 90 percent of the states with the United States are working to offset deficits, with some even squandering their tobacco settlement funds in the process?

At what point do people really get concerned? Scared? Panicked? Where is the trigger point when people lose confidence in the economy and emotional selling strikes world financial markets? At what point do consumers tap out for the lack of job growth and the fear of layoff? No one is sure. Third-party candidate Ross Perot garnered 20 percent of the popular vote for president in 1992 with his charts and graphs on the potential catastrophe of government debt, and that was 12 years ago. The figures are higher now. A lot higher.

Some economists assure us that debt, as a percentage of GDP, is manageable. Free traders point out that major exporting countries to the United States, like China and Japan, will subsidize U.S. budget deficits because the U.S. consumer market is so important to them. But can the United States count on continued growth in the new business normal, and does it want foreign countries ending up owning most of its government obligations? The United States is already a debtor nation, which means it owes more as a country to foreign nations than it owns of their obligations.

Other economists point out that the trade deficit, so widely reported in popular media, does not tell the whole story. The reported deficit figures are for merchandise only. The United States has a substantial surplus in the buying and selling of ser-

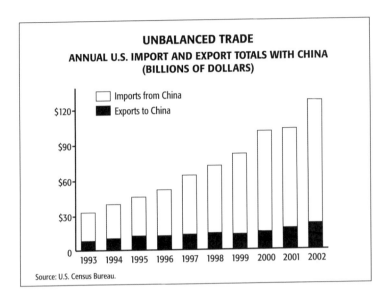

UNBALANCED TRADE
ANNUAL U.S. IMPORT AND EXPORT TOTALS WITH CHINA
(BILLIONS OF DOLLARS)

☐ Imports from China
■ Exports to China

Source: U.S. Census Bureau.

vices between countries. This fact is almost never reported and is largely unknown. Unfortunately, it is of small consequence because the merchandise deficit overwhelms the surplus in services. A barrel of oil sells for about $50 at this writing. As oil rises in cost, it worsens the U.S. merchandise trade figures because the United States imports more oil than it produces. What if oil goes to $60 or $70 per barrel? It's your call because few forecasters even saw a $50 price. This you can be sure: ballooning U.S. merchandise trade deficits will weaken the dollar. A weak dollar causes the value of U.S. government notes and bonds to decline. Interest rates will have to rise to attract continued buying by Japan and China to finance the national debt. If they stop, you can write and date your own scenario to the calamity.

We have lived with debt all our lives. Debt is not new, and it is not all "knee-jerk" bad. But the numbers keep getting bigger, and the horizon is red. In the past, we have been able to grow the economy away from debt problems. But the rules are different today in the new business normal. Moralists, environmentalists, fiscal conservatives, liberals, and even economists actively debate the merits of technological growth. Economic growth is no longer a given. Everyone is waiting for the "next big thing": computers, wireless communication, the Internet—what's next?

The new business normal is the feeling that business confidence in the long term is lagging. The Dow Jones Industrial Average has done little in five years. A majority of the population feels the country is headed in the wrong direction. For the first

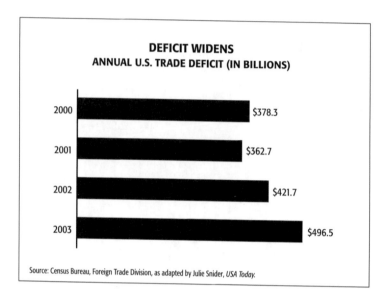

DEFICIT WIDENS
ANNUAL U.S. TRADE DEFICIT (IN BILLIONS)

2000	$378.3
2001	$362.7
2002	$421.7
2003	$496.5

Source: Census Bureau, Foreign Trade Division, as adapted by Julie Snider, *USA Today.*

time, some parents feel their children will be worse off than they were. In many industries, profits are up and productivity is up, but sales growth is hard to realize. There are patches of optimism, spurred by supereasy monetary and fiscal policies (debt creation). Yet a broader look finds that peak-to-peak and valley-to-valley sales trends are down. Debt seems more of a burden despite low interest costs. Capital spending must have traceable and short-term lines to increased profitability, or the money stays in the bank. Hiring takes place only if more orders have been booked. There are spurts of demand, but in the new business normal, sustained organic growth is no longer predictable. Companies are pursuing mergers and acquisition as a primary growth strategy.

It is true that corporate balance sheets have strengthened. But this has occurred mostly through restructuring, refinancing, and equity swaps. There is little corporate pricing power in the global economy for all but the strongest brands. In turn, companies face hard choices in how they meet their obligations and simultaneously grow their businesses. Rising debt burdens of governments are constricting public spending programs. Consumers are tapping their major source of wealth creation, home equity, to maintain their lifestyle and fulfill obligations. The risk of not being able to pay back borrowed capital from operations, personal income, and tax revenues is growing.

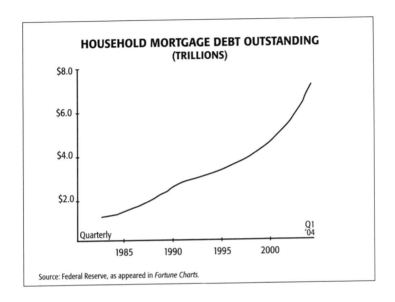

Source: Federal Reserve, as appeared in *Fortune Charts*.

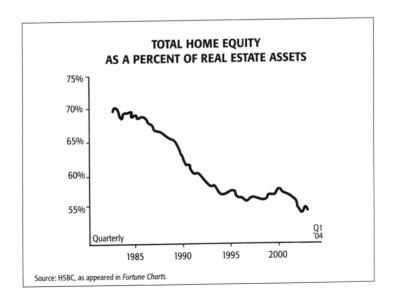

Source: HSBC, as appeared in *Fortune Charts*.

Given all this, and while we await the next "big thing," are there any marketing opportunities in the fog of growing debt burdens? As you ponder the new business normal, here are a few thoughts. I would begin by looking at health care and education. These are the only two industries in the past 40-some years where product selling prices have risen above the rate of inflation. Pricing power is evident. Both industries have a positive correlation with the demographic trends previously discussed. Health care relates quantitatively and qualitatively to the aging of the population. Adult education, worker training, and immigrant schooling are dynamic themes in education. Knowledge management is a corporate differentiator in the new business normal.

Another avenue of thought is for private companies to increasingly look to take over public functions. Deficit-plagued governments are outsourcing services to private firms that can perform them more efficiently. One example is the U.S. Mail Service using FedEx logistics for expedited mail and package delivery. Privately run schools and prisons have precedent. Outsourcing government services is an expanding market opportunity from systems management to knowledge services.

A successful sales proposition for high-tech companies is one where suppliers look to their customers for opportunities to trade capital costs for direct costs. If a supplier can provide services as a direct cost to the customer, with the result being a reduction in the customer's requirement for capital assets, the proposition will often be evaluated. Supplier-owned infrastructure and supplier-managed systems in areas of industrial gas delivery, pure water maintenance, or chemicals disposal are common in high tech. This approach reduces capital funding, which usually means it reduces debt incursion and debt service costs. It also shortens the customer's capital payback period and relieves the customer of maintaining knowledge and technical proficiency in specialized support areas. The customer has a known direct cost figure for budgeting and relies on operational skill to produce margin.

Professional service providers need to further detail service opportunities where customer proximity is required and where knowledge preempts cost as a competitive factor. While product prices are under pressure due to low-cost foreign labor and relatively cheap foreign currencies, professional service costs remain buoyant because there are no imported substitutes for most professional services. Outsourcing of routine professional and white-collar services is on the rise, but outsourcing can't exist in the new business normal, where customer or client proximity is required.

Demographics and debt are subjects on center stage because they are real factors in the new business normal. The next "big thing" is only a probability, however amply supported by historical precedent. Continuing to go forward through technical innovation is crucial to keeping our future from drowning. Technological breakthroughs of the magnitude of antibiotics, telephones, television, or the Internet are needed to lessen the impact of debt, budget deficits, and the exodus of perhaps millions of jobs. The United States' very ability to thrive as a country depends on it. There has been no better engine to create jobs, develop new industries, and raise levels of living than through technological home runs. In the meantime, as the world keeps its collective head down in R&D pursuits, the new business normal will remain a disruptive challenge for years to come for the unwary and the unprepared.

Large print available at a slight up charge. Cash only, please.

TWELVE

Is the New Business Normal Sustainable?

"Thus the reason the farsighted ruler and his superior commander conquer the enemy at every move, and achieve successes far beyond the reach of the common crowd, is foreknowledge. Such foreknowledge cannot be had from ghosts and spirits, educed by comparison with past events, or verified by astrological calculations. It must come from people—people who know the enemy's situation."

> —Sun Tzu (*The Art of Warfare*, translation with an introduction and commentary by Roger Ames, [New York: Balantine Books, 1993])

In writing this book, it quickly became apparent that fundamental changes in the business world have converged to create a new environment for companies either global or planning to become global. The critical factor common to these changes is the adoption speed and proliferation of technical development. Technology does not go backward—it only ramifies. The number

Demographics

AVERAGE FAMILY SIZE
UNITED STATES
(PEOPLE PER FAMILY)

YEAR	PEOPLE PER FAMILY (AVG)
1960	3.67
1970	3.58
1980	3.29
1990	3.17
2000	3.17
2010 E	3.15 E

Source: U.S. Census Bureau.

Debt

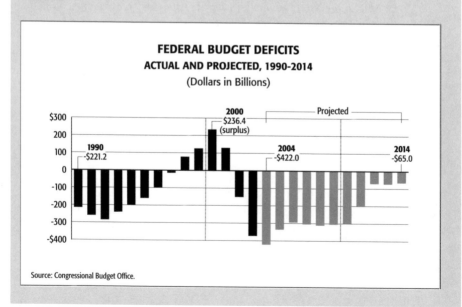

FEDERAL BUDGET DEFICITS
ACTUAL AND PROJECTED, 1990-2014
(Dollars in Billions)

Source: Congressional Budget Office.

and types of discoveries, the rapid development of applications, and subsequent commercialization are happening at exponential rates. This pace will neither diminish nor reverse course. Knowledge exposed is knowledge eternal.

Not covered in the book are things over which we have little control (but can influence in some small way). For example, the certainty of global warming is a part of the new business normal environment, but its impact is highly uncertain. What is known is that the unthinkable possibility of a major change in climate over a short period of time is now thinkable and is reported in *An Abrupt Climate Change Scenario and Its Implications for United States National Security*, by Peter Schwartz and Doug Randall.

It appears that the coming apart of civilizations at cultural borders will continue for the foreseeable future and will be an unpredictable risk to commerce the world over. One can only hope that the Muslim reformation will proceed with less bloodshed and be over sooner than the one Christianity went through. The disruption to global economics remains a potential threat.

There are eight civilizations on the planet. Seven are non-western. This is worthy of more than a little thought by leaders of companies with global reach.

Covered, but worthy of iteration, is the continuing threat of a global financial crisis brought about by either of the physical influences mentioned or by the financial system itself. We have covered some of the potential triggers; however, the one looming largest is the concentration and influence of foreign holdings of the ever-enlarging U.S. national debt. The consequences of debt will be minimized by the U.S. government as long as the economy keeps growing. A period of no growth puts it in uncharted waters.

New Products

"Most of the innovation in our industry (high tech) has been driven by fairly large companies. Take IBM. IBM invented the disk drive, core memory, and fractal geometry. IBM has been a cornucopia of invention." —Larry Ellison, CEO, Oracle Corp. (*Business Week*, "The Future of Tech–Roadblocks," Aug. 25, 2003)

Frameworks: A Story from Honda

Honda was trying to develop the CVCC engine, which had lower emissions and higher fuel efficiency. Souichiro Honda, the founder and then CEO of Honda, one day told his engineers that the engine would finally give Honda the opportunity to beat the big three.

The engineers looked at Mr. Honda and said, "Please, don't say such a thing. We are not doing this to beat the other guys. We are doing this for our children."

Mr. Honda was ashamed of himself, said that he realized that he had become too old, and decided to retire.

So are the changes of the new business normal truly irrevocable and sustainable? And if so, what can you do about it?

A few of the themes of permanent change covered in this book can provide insight.

Speed

Look at microprocessors, now at multigigahertz speeds. Look at the acceleration performance (0 to 60 mph) of standard automobiles. Look at instant communication of voice and data. Look at e-commerce, where clicks have replaced bricks. Look at the Internet. Look at product development and obsolescence cycles.

There are new technologies in our world that are about to change our lives and work in revolutionary ways, some sooner than others. *Technology Review*, February 2004, has given us a snapshot of these innovative fields. Where will the centers of commercial development be in the emerging technologies of universal translation, synthetic biology, nanowires, Bayseian machine learning, t-rays, distributed storage, RNA interference, power grid control, microfluidic optical fibers, and personal geonomics?

China

"Fast economic growth is generally regarded as more important than local ownership. Interested foreign companies must stake a considerable claim now if they want to be in China at all. Already GE has over 300 purchasing agents in the country who certify suppliers for global sourcing. In 2004, more Buicks will likely be sold in China than in the United States. Its markets evolve quickly. The market's challenge is that profits must often be reinvested to maintain market position."

The McKinsey Quarterly. "A Guide to Doing Business in China," pp. 37-45, 2004.

Intangible Assets: Patents

Patent activity at the U.S. Patent and Trademark Office is rising.

Year	U.S. Applications	U.S. Grants	Non-U.S. Applications	Non-U.S. Grants
1994	107,233	56,066	82,624	45,610
2003	188,941	87,901	154,500	81,127

The United Nation's World Intellectual Property Organization membership has increased from 171 in 1994 to 181 in 2003. Patent activity has increased in almost all industrialized countries as a direct proportion to their GDP.

Intangible Assets: Market Leadership

"The power of market leadership is just enormous. Big companies with lots of customers have advantages. But, those advantages disappear very rapidly if you're a follower and not a leader." —Roger McNamee (*Business Week*, "The Future of Tech–Roadblocks," Aug. 25, 2003)

Globalization

Brands are available anywhere, anytime. Sourcing is global for any company regardless of size or location. National currencies are giving way to continental currencies. Global currencies are next (i.e., Visa is just a mechanism). Economic agreements among regional nations are the norm. The concerted policy direction of world governments is to reduce and eliminate tariffs around the globe. The expectation of the consumer is to have the right to acquire the goods and services that meet individual needs regardless of the source. The attractiveness of global cooperation among companies to gain scale, scope, speed, and persistence in chosen markets remains unabated.

Important demographic patterns are reshaping markets and organizational thinking. The only possible detour would be by governments that are benevolent or malevolent. While science maintains active life longer and having fewer children is gaining in economic reality, overall demographic trends will remain strong and catalytic for global business.

So What Can You Do?

As a company, start by objectively establishing a good understanding of where you are today so you can calibrate what needs to be accomplished in the future. Start with a review of your domain and make an up-to-date statement describing it. Then, determine your competitive position. Know what being "the best" means in terms of the whole customer experience. Look at the IT systems your company employs and rate them with respect to how fast and effectively you can respond to a customer problem or business opportunity anywhere in the world.

Streamlining

"The ability to wring out incremental gains in quality improvements, efficiency improvements and technological improvements is United Technologies Corp greatest strengths." —George David, CEO, UTC (*Business Week*, Oct. 25, 2004)

Streamlining
Critical Mass: Rule of Three

The Global Big Three

Advertising Agencies:
Publicis Groupe SA ADS
Omnicom Group Inc.
Interpublic GR OF COS

Airline alliances:
Star Alliance
One World Alliance
Sky Team

Beverage companies:
Coca-Cola
Pepsi
Diageo

Defense contractors:
Lockheed Martin Corp.
Boeing Co.
BAE Systems

Food producers:
Unilever N.V.
ConAgra Foods
IBP Inc.

Medical supply
   companies:
Abbott Laboratories
Baxter International Inc.
Becton, Dickinson & Co.

Mining companies:
BHP LTD
Rio Tinto plc ADR
Cameco Corp.

Shipbuilders:
Todd Shipyards Corp.
Anagel-Amer
   Shipbuilding
Conrad Industries Inc.

Steel companies:
Corus Group plc
Pohang Iron & Steel ADS
USX-U.S. Steel Group

Tobacco companies:
Philip Morris
Japan Tobacco
British American
   Tobacco

Toy makers:
Mattel Inc.
Hasbro Inc.
Electronic Arts, Inc.

Jagdish Sheth and Rajendra Sisodia. *The Rule of Three* (New York: The Free Press, 2002)

Streamline

Next, measure your company's financial reach and risk tolerance to assess the need to share development risk and margin with partners. Closely allied is an assessment of your technical competency both in product functionality and process efficiency. Determine the compatibility of your technical competency with the overall goals of your business plan and strategy, and set forth initiatives to reconcile any incompatibility.

Decide whether your procedural systems streamline the company and whether they will be capable of doing so in the future. Ask yourself whether capabilities in systems and procedures in such areas as quality measurement and control, new product development, and customer response are streamlined and working to benefit the customer. Are systems serving their business purpose without being burdened by unnecessary costs and administrative priorities? Can the entire system respond to real-time data and information for rapid decision making? Based on the elements of the new business normal that most affect you, ascertain what your systems must be capable of to deliver the experience desired by the customer in the future.

Leadership

Because leadership in the new business normal is at a high premium, measuring executive talent will be an ongoing challenge. The basis for selection will be a person's fitness for managing the elements of the new business normal rather than his or her company loyalty, time in grade, age, and, to some extent, the experience gained in the company. For example, the experience value of heading manufacturing operations will diminish if the company elects to outsource production. The new business normal is such a point of departure that effective leadership will not necessarily come from those who have enjoyed the prosperity of the company's past because prosperity in the new business normal comes from a different landscape. Those belonging to a generation (as used here, not age related) of experiences common to the past could very well be hamstrung by their own emotional equity in a company's history and patterns of past success. Success tends to validate what a person has thought and done. But past success cannot be readily extrapolated into the new business normal because the environment is vastly different.

Knowledge Management: U.S. Navy

"Bringing the knowledge of the department (of the Navy) to the tip of the spear"

"The Navy has gone full-speed ahead in adapting knowledge practices and processes. There is no company in the world anywhere near it in scope, and it's a very balanced endeavor. They are talking about people, technology and social relationships that make things work." — Larry Prusak, executive director of IBM's Institute for Knowledge Management in Cambridge, Mass.

As a starting point, select a director's committee to inventory your combined leadership skills as a management team, and compare those to what will be needed in the new business normal environment. Assess your organizational structure to see whether it is set up to deliver the experiences and technologies needed by the customer in the future. The overarching questions are: where are we in developing leaders capable of dealing with the new business normal and how are we going to close the gap?

Market Position

Rationalize your market position in terms of your importance in a market and your ability to influence the growth and prosperity of that market. Select the customers who will emerge as, or who are, the dominant innovative leaders, and examine whether you can deliver what they will need. For example, can you support 15 percent R&D expenditures annually? Do you possess the core competencies needed to deliver the whole customer experience?

Once you know where you are relative to your domain, competitive position, systems development, leadership development, financial reach, technical competency, and critical mass, you must set a vision that is not esoteric (e.g., being the "best in the world" or growing at X percent per year) but specific in terms of setting forth the future requirements of customers and an organizational model of how they will access those requirements from you. Will they access through e-commerce? Will the services be designed into the product? Will suppliers retain ownership of everything but the product's experience in use? What road map of incremental differentiating features will be required in future models?

Government Learning Objectives
for KM Certification

1. Have knowledge of the value added by Knowledge Management to the business proposition, including the return on investment, performance measures, and the ability to develop a business case.

2. Have knowledge of the strategies and processes to transfer explicit and tacit knowledge across time, space and organizational boundaries, including retrieval of critical archived information. This transfer has a spiraling nature, i.e., ideas build on ideas, and old ideas may or may not be of current value.

3. Have knowledge of state-of-the-art and evolving technology solutions that promote KM, including portals and collaborative and distributed learning technologies.

4. Have knowledge of and the ability to facilitate knowledge creation, sharing and reuse. This includes developing partnerships and alliances, designing creative knowledge spaces, and using incentive structures.

5. Have knowledge of learning styles and behaviors, strive for continuous improvement and be actively engaged in exploring new ideas and concepts.

6. Have working knowledge of state-of-the-art research and implementation strategies for knowledge management, information management, document and records management and data management. This includes project management of knowledge initiatives and retrieval of critical archived information.

7. Have understanding of the global and economic importance of developing knowledge-based organizations to meet the challenges of the knowledge era.

8. Have the ability to use systems thinking in implementing solutions.

9. Have the ability to design, develop and sustain communities of interest and practice.

10. Have the ability to design, develop and sustain the flow of knowledge. This includes understanding the breakthrough skills needed to leverage virtual teamwork and the effective use of social networks.

11. Have the ability to perform cultural and ethnographic analyses, develop knowledge taxonomies, facilitate knowledge audits, and perform knowledge mapping and needs assessments.

12. Have the ability to capture, evaluate and use best-known practices, including the use of storytelling to transfer these best practices.

13. Have the ability to manage change and complex knowledge initiatives and projects.

14. Have the ability to identify customers and stakeholders and tie organizational goals to the needs and requirements of those customers and stakeholders.

Key Elements

With gained clarity about your current levels of organizational development and your vision in terms of customer requirements, you will need to think through your leadership approaches to the most challenging management elements of the new business normal. Put the highest priority on these elements, and charge the board with their stewardship. Make these elements part of strategic planning as guides, screens, and goals along with making them part of your incentive and reward system.

China
Systems and processes
Innovation
Corporate governance and executive selection
Brand management
Knowledge management
Customer relationships

Activities you can organize and undertake to better prepare yourself to understand and succeed:

- Stay informed, educated, and current. Easier said than done, but remember that knowledge management is the essence of competing successfully.
- Assign your staff to write white papers on the above elements of the new business normal addressing approaches and applications in your business environment.
- Schedule offsite conferences that focus on creating consensus around values, lexicons, and leadership styles.
- Develop organizational and corporate models that examine cost, process disciplines, customer satisfaction, functional accountability, and the attainment of tomorrow.

Leadership

"There are very, very few people who can lead one of the major international companies, and you have to pay what the market demands."
—Charles Peck, compensation specialist for the Conference Board

Finding people with near expert levels of technical, financial, and legal experience who show good character has grown to near crisis levels; travel is up for those individuals to as high as 80 percent, and finding the ones willing to work and live in an environment where a single misstatement can lead to a jail sentence is getting more expensive. Development programs for leaders are rampant, and the modus operandi is to have any number of people coming up the organization at any one time. These emerging and potential leaders are actively managed to expose them to cultures, operating disciplines, technologies, and the company's entire business community while inculcating them in the company's values. It is a problem that no responsible oversight group takes lightly. Not just governance but executive selection. Management often has too narrow a set of criteria to adequately address the requirements of next generation (not age generation but mind-set and experience generation—generation as used here is independent of age, tenure, and loyalty) skills needed to understand and succeed in the new business normal. In the new business normal, boards will have to become more engaged in the oversight of the executive development and placement activities of the company or risk facing a leadership crisis.

The number-one responsibility of any executive leadership team is the survival of the company over time. In the new business normal, mistakes and mismanagement will be fatal.

Some Parting Thoughts

- The realities of the new business normal are harsh, demanding, and entrenched. Companies that survive will enjoy a rate and level of commerce and prosperity that are probably unprecedented. Successful managements of the new business normal will be celebrated and accorded the same wealth and status now given to top entertainers.

- Management careers will be rich in diversity and opportunity and fulfilling as corporations take on greater societal roles.

- A successful CEO is a likely candidate for leadership in state and national government. Instead of courthouses and senate chambers, government leadership in the new business normal may well emerge from the executive suites. Competition among nations (read warfare) will be based on economics. Who is better prepared for that kind of war than an executive from the new business normal? Economic and business skills will trump political skills.

Corporations will become more engaged and responsible for societal issues such as global warming, environmental degradation, cultural tolerance, and wealth distribution. As global leaders, they will have the opportunity to foster behaviors that respect human dignity and encourage the achievement of fundamental human rights. Public accountability for corporations will grow in proportion to their size and economic prominence. If corporations are mindful of the legacy they leave to humankind as a prime measure of their intrinsic value, they will have served the new business normal well.

Those uncomfortable with the realities of the new business normal run the risk of being a recipient of the corporate Darwin awards. Adaptation will be rewarded with survival. In the end, if anything, I have understated the speed, magnitude, and pervasiveness of the new business normal.

Prepare yourself, and enjoy the journey.

May others benefit from your lead.

BIBLIOGRAPHY AND SUGGESTED READING

Chopra, Deepak. *The Soul of Leadership.* Kellogg School of Management Executive Program, Oct. 2003.

Collins, Jim. *Good to Great.* New York: HarperCollins, 2001.

Csorba, Les T. *Trust: The One Thing That Makes or Breaks a Leader.* Nashville: Thomas Nelson, Inc., 2004.

Gates, Bill. *Business @ the Speed of Thought: Succeeding in the Digital Economy.* New York: Warner Books, 1999.

Ghyczy, Tiha von. *Clausewitz on Strategy.* New York: John Wiley & Sons, Inc., 2001.

Hamel, Gary and Liisa Valikangas. *The Quest for Resilience.* Harvard Business Review, Sept., 2003.

Huntington, Samuel P. *The Clash of Civilizations and the Remaking of World Order.* New York: Touchstone, 1996.

Jennings, Ken and John Stahl-Wert. 2003. *The Serving Leader.* San Francisco: Berrett-Koehler, 2003.

Kluge, Jurgen, Wolfram Stein, and Thomas Licht. *Knowledge Unplugged.* The McKinsey Global Survey on Knowledge Management.

Kushner, Harold S. *Living a Life That Matters.* New York: Anchor Books, 2001.

Mowen, John C., and Mike Minor. *Consumer Behavior: A Framework.* Pearson Education, 2000.

Sheth, Jagdish and Rajendra Sisodia. *The Rule of Three.* New York: The Free Press, 2002.

Smith, Preston G. *Developing Products in Half the Time: New Rules, New Tools.* New York: John Wiley & Sons, Inc., 1998.

Sullivan, Gordon R. *Hope Is not a Method.* New York: Broadway Books, 1996.

Tzu, Sun. *The Art of War.* London, Oxford University Press, 1963.

Ubæk, Uffe. *Kaos Pilot A-Z.* Aarhus, Denmark: KaosCommunication, 2003.

Wheatley, Margaret. *Leadership and the New Science.* San Francisco: Barrett-Koehler Publisher, Inc., 1999.

ABOUT THE AUTHORS

Michael W. Wright

Michael W. Wright passionately believes that large corporations today have a responsibility to ensure their value systems and responsibilities extend from respecting and protecting the companies they lead to respecting and protecting the very fabric of the world we live in. Developed in large part during his 25 years of high tech industry experience while on a quest to understand the ever-occurring changes in business this passion brings forth a desire to explore with others what he has learned.

Wright's experience spans multiple roles and industries. He is currently the president and chief operating officer of Entegris, Inc. a publicly held, global high technology company. The company is the leading provider of materials integrity management to the semiconductor, microelectronics, life sciences and fuel cell industries. His broad range of leadership roles covers executive positions ranging from CEO, COO, Executive VP, VP of Marketing and Sales. These roles were at such semiconductor related flagship companies as Integrated Air Systems, General Signal (GCA, Ultratech), Integrated Solutions and Empak. Wright has participated in industries from instrumentation, filtration, lithography, materials,and software. During his close association with SEMATECH, he founded Wright Williams and Kelly, the largest provider of cost-of-ownership software and operational cost modeling tools for the semiconductor and other high technology industries.

His extensive business travels have taken him across North America, Europe, Russia, Japan, China, and Asia, where he has gained insights into and appreciation of the values, methods and mores of the global marketplace. He knows China, Taiwan, Russia, and Japan the most intimately with two decades experience in sales, marketing, partnerships and joint ventures. Most importantly, he has nurtured the relationships necessary to do business in those countries.

Wright has developed a strategic savvy over the years for the positioning, marketing, branding, and tactical execution needed for competing in the global environment of high technology products. He has authored numerous articles, and has chaired the Semiconductor Equipment and Materials International (SEMI) annual North American Industry Strategy Symposium (ISS). Wright serves on the August Technologies, Starview Technologies and Minnesota High Tech Association boards of directors.

Michael's success in developing strategies and setting the right course to travel in the business world are reflected in his favorite hobbies of photography and sailing.

ABOUT THE AUTHORS

Walter J. Ferguson

To get a true measure of the life rich with extraordinary experiences contributing author Walter J. Ferguson has lived, take a look at the places he's been to in the world, the names hanging on his wall at home and the simple, but meaningful philosophies he'll throw your way.

His travels? To Guatemala, Costa Rica, Thailand, Japan, Great Britain, Germany, Switzerland, Italy, Malaysia, Singapore and Taiwan. Ferguson has traveled and done business in all of these countries, as well as at home in the United States. From his 15 years of sales and marketing experience for Fortune 500 companies, to being president of two Silicon Valley companies— EKC Technology and Dryden Engineering and as executive liaison between the historical Crocker family of San Francisco and their many enterprises— Ferguson has run the gamut of industrial experiences that bring both a little spark and spice to his contributions to this book, *The New Business Normal*.

Famous names on the wall? John Foster Dulles, William Fargo, J.P. Morgan, Leland Stanford and Rose Kennedy—one of the great U.S. Secretaries of State, the namesake of Wells Fargo, perhaps the greatest business tycoon in American history, the founder of Stanford University, and the Grand Dame of the Camelot of 20th Century American politics. One of Ferguson's favorite hobbies is collecting cancelled stock certificates of historic value going back to the late 18th century, including the original signed certificates of these American icons.

Philosophies? The customer is the primary source of learning in business. Learning is lifelong. Customers and markets are the prism for organizing growth. Dare to be excellent. Integrity is everything. Simple, but meaningful messages that have guided Walter through a fascinating and successful career, and impacted so many whose paths he has crossed over the years.

Ferguson decided to contribute to this book because helping clients, customers and colleagues has always been the most satisfying part of his business life. This work is simply a natural extension of that belief. And thanks to Ferguson's invaluable contributions to *The New Business Normal*, it is hoped this book will help light the way for others who are, or will be, traveling down the roads of life and business around the world.